The Cellar-House of Pervyse

"THE TWO"

The Cellar-House of Pervyse

The Incredible Account of
Two Nurses on the Western Front
During the Great War

G. E. Mitton

LEONAUR

The Cellar-House of Pervyse
The Incredible Account of
Two Nurses on the Western Front
During the Great War
by G. E. Mitton

First published under the title
The Cellar-House of Pervyse

Leonaur is an imprint of Oakpast Ltd

Copyright in this form © 2011 Oakpast Ltd

ISBN: 978-0-85706-557-5 (hardcover)
ISBN: 978-0-85706-558-2 (softcover)

http://www.leonaur.com

Publisher's Notes

Contents

To the
Splendid Belgian Soldiers
Whom We Have Learnt to Love

Note

Of all the things told of the Great War surely this is the most uncommon, that two women should have been at the front with the Belgian Army almost from the beginning. That they should have lived as the soldiers lived, caring for them, tending them, taking cocoa and soup into the trenches and even to the outposts. And this is what has been done by two British ladies. Both young themselves, one very young, they yet have mothered Belgian soldiers through their trials and made a centre of light and comfort for the soldiers bereft of all that makes life dear and often in agonized uncertainty as to where their wives, mothers, or children might be. In March, 1915, a very stern decree was passed by the allied armies at Paris to the effect that no women should be allowed in the firing-line, but an exception was made in the case of these two, mentioned by name, because they had proved themselves.

How did they begin? I have often been asked that. The book answers. What did they do? The book answers that too. They lived at first for long months in a cellar twelve feet by ten, they slept on straw, and of necessity used foul water from a ditch. As the village they were in was under constant shell-fire, the chauffeurs, and sometimes wounded soldiers, had to sleep in that cellar too. There was, of course, no possibility of changing clothes; they lay down as they were, and were often called up in the middle of the night to attend to ghastly wounds. They had none of the appliances and conveniences surgeons think necessary; there was the greatest difficulty even in getting boiling water for sterilizing any instruments which had to be used in first-aid.

The air was heavy with the smell of antiseptics and decayed matter and worse! Night after night the guns roared before and behind—their own and the enemies'. There was no minute night or day when swift death might not pounce upon them. Their clothes were stained with soup and cocoa and smears of blood, their hands got engrained with coarse work—washing, cutting up, and peeling potatoes for the soup, potatoes which they had often grubbed up from neighbouring farms under fire.

They sacrificed their hair, for it was impossible to retain long hair in such conditions. Thrice they were shelled out and left without a roof over their heads. When the cellar became uninhabitable they removed to a house further up the village, which the Engineers made up with sand-bags, but it was not very long before the Germans got the range of this and smashed half of it down, burying a row of young dead boys who had been brought in past aid and laid out on the verandah. Then these indomitable women went over to England; they lectured, they told the public of their work, and the public responded. They came back with funds.

Up to this time they had paid entirely for themselves with the aid of private friends. They built a wooden hut further back from the trenches, and they had not been in it three days before enormous shells thundered around, and there was nothing between their beloved wounded and death but a roof of match-boarding, so they moved further back still. But they could not rest there; it was at the trenches they were needed to save the lives of those who were so overcome by shock that to carry them any distance over those smashed-up roads meant death, whereas rest and warmth and care for even a few hours gave them the strength to make a fight for their lives. So back the two women went to the shattered village, now more desolate than ever. With their own hands they piled up sand-bags, working at night, going in from their further post after a heavy day's work with the wounded and sick. Then they settled again in the village, and there they still carry on the work.

But it has not been unrecognized, for King Albert had heard and seen what they had done, how many lives they had saved, and how they had inspired the worn soldiers with their own bright courage; so he sent for them and pinned on their khaki tunics the Knights' Cross of the Order of Leopold II., which carries with it the right to have the Belgian soldiers present arms. He personally thanked them for all they had endured. And reward came in another way, because Mrs. Knocker, a young widow, met out there the young Baron Harold de T'Serclaes belonging to one of the oldest Belgian families. It was almost a case of love at first sight, and after the many difficulties incidental to the bride and bridegroom's belonging to different nations had been overcome, they were married, and both continue to carry on their duties just the same. It is a wonderful tale.

That it has been written is due to the suggestion of Major A . A. Gordon, M. V.O., who, since taking part in the siege of, and retreat from, Antwerp, has gone backwards and forwards regularly from England to within a few miles of Pervyse. He had seen the Two in their posts from the days of the cellar at Pervyse through their varied vicissitudes; he had seen Mrs. Knocker (as she was then) standing with the skirt of her tunic holed with shrapnel; he knew something of what she and her companion had had to endure of dirt, discomfort, and actual want; he had known what it meant to drive up the long straight road to Pervyse when the shells hurtled around. Fully appreciating the splendour and romance of this strange life lived so quietly and untheatrically from day to day and month to month, he persuaded the Two to entrust him with their journals and to let him have their home letters, 'so that the tale which they had written down quite simply as a record for themselves in the years to come might be made accessible also to others.

It is doubtful if they would have allowed it to be done but for their earnest devotion to the wounded Belgian soldiers, and the hope that the book might inspire interest in them in the hearts of a wider circle than their own personal appeal could reach. So the matter came into my hands in the shape of little fat, mud-stained books, written in pencil at odd moments, sometimes even under fire as one or the other sat in a car waiting to convey wounded men to a hospital. As one of them says in one of these journals, "that's the hardest part of all; it requires nerve to drive an ambulance steadily under fire, but to sit still doing nothing with the shells bursting around takes it out of you worst of all."

I should like to emphasize the fact that these journals have not been in any way touched up before they came to me; they were just as they had been written. Plain, bald facts are put down simply, and because of their very simplicity they carry con-viction as to the writers' single-mindedness. Not once throughout is there any personal complaint, any whining; these journals are not used as safety-valves for feeling. After the record of some terrible experience, the comments, if any, are always, "How brave these soldiers are!" "What a terrible time for the poor soldiers !" Never for themselves, the writers.

The facts are so astounding that they need no dressing. My part has been merely that of a recorder, running the two parallel journals together and omitting repetitions or details too small to be of general interest. But I am sure that among the multitude of books written of what has happened at the front there is not one that will remain longer in the minds of those who read them than this of the heroic Two of Pervyse.

G. E. Mitton.

September, 1916.

CHAPTER 1

The Start

I shall never forget them as I saw them first, a little oddly mixed group. They might have been a party of Cook's tourists going for a weekend across the Channel as they stood there in Victoria Station; but it was more than a weekend trip they had to face. At first I thought that some of them were merely seeing the others off, especially the lady with cherries in her hat. In fact, there were only two who looked real sportswomen, and they were Mrs. Knocker and Mairi Chisholm. They were dressed in big khaki overcoats, but as these were flung open one could see the high boots and tunics underneath, and there was no manner of doubt that they were wearing knickerbocker khaki suits in London! The others were slightly scandalized—one could see it in their furtive glances, and the way they obviously avoided looking just where the khaki knickers were.

We are so funny, we English; there is nothing so deeply ingrained in us as a horror of any sort of attitudinizing, and we are so much afraid of it that we will not get ready for the moment lest the moment should not come. It was little more than a month then since war had broken out, and still we were rather shamefaced about it, most of us; even the recruits felt a little foolish doing those queer exercises in public, as if they might be ridiculous and not really wanted at the front after all. Thus, of course, it was difficult for these gentle ladies, who wore correct costumes and picture hats, to think there could really be any need for stepping right outside the conventional lines, at all events until they got to the war zone. The question how it was to be done afterwards had not come within their horizon.

Then there were the men of the party. One, a most heroic *padre*, had gone in for the whole thing. He never considered for a moment whether he looked ridiculous or not; he was a most single-minded, upright gentleman, as he proved many a time afterwards; but the clergy are not as a rule notorious for the cut of their clothes, and he had not been able to afford the expense of an officer's khaki suit, so his was a ready-made rough Tommy's costume, serviceable enough, and it fell into the picture very completely when he "got there."

Men's clothes have this advantage over women's, they are at all events more practical, and the two clever London doctors who were going out for the sake of the experience looked very comfortable in their loose-fitting tweeds the suits they wore when golfing at the week-ends. As for the leader of the party himself, well, he was different from anyone; he never had cared a button about his clothes, and would have handled wounded men in a frock-coat and top-hat without a care in the world. His hat was as often on wrong side as not, for his excessive carelessness about dress seemed to culminate in his headgear, and a cheap cyclist's check cap would do for him as well as a Belgian officer's gold-tasselled cap.

What matter? He was a visionary, full of enthusiasm, and but for him this group of people, some of whom at least were to distinguish themselves in self-sacrificing and noble work with the Belgian Army, would never have been able to go out at all. That the doctor did not combine in himself opposite virtues was no fault of his—who does? He had a positively heroic disregard for detail; it was all one to him if his corps consisted of two members or of fifteen, as it actually did. I verily believe if I, a Londoner, with no experience whatever of medicine or surgery, had stepped forward at the minute the engine-whistle sounded, and said, "May I also come with you as a member of your corps?" he would have hauled me into the gathering speed of the train by one arm, and said, "Dear friend, yes, certainly; by all means!"

It was characteristic of him that he had managed to start the corps by a fluke. He had seen Mrs. Knocker on a motor-cycle doing despatch work for the Women's Emergency Corps, and with a stroke of genius had recognized that she was the one woman who could help him in the ambulance work he burned to do in Belgium. He was quite right about that. A more highly efficient woman could hardly have been found. Most women do difficult technical things now, but few did them before the war. Mrs. Knocker was a fully trained nurse, an excellent mechanic and chauffeur; she spoke French and German, and with all that it hardly needs adding she was a capable woman; but the genius of Dr. Munro lay in recognizing it, because she doesn't look like this, or at any rate not like the stereotyped notion of a woman who can do all these things.

She is a little above medium height, very slightly built, with a beautiful profile, clear complexion, and singularly bright hazel eyes. When you look at her eyes you see at once that she is full of sensibility and very easily hurt in fact, she is the kind of woman who would really take it to heart if, in a great emergency, you swore at her! She minds very much what her relations to her fellow-beings are, and this constitutes just the difference between the woman who can communicate vital energy to wounded men so as to set them on their feet again and the woman who, however efficient as a nurse she may be, remains outside the personality of her patients.

To Mrs. Knocker Dr. Munro had confided the choosing of the rest of the corps, and the first member of it she had selected was a capital Scottish girl called Mairi Chisholm. Though Mairi hailed from Inverness originally, she had recently lived in Devon near Mrs. Knocker. They had been friends before the war, and ridden motor-cycles together, and it was shrewd Mairi who had christened her friend "Gipsy," a name which suits her down to the ground, and is so much more suitable than her own hard married name (which, however, she no longer possesses) that I shall henceforth use it.

When the war began Gipsy and Mairi had immediately come up to London and offered their services to the War Office as despatch-riders. You see, Gipsy has vision, and though at that time the idea that women could do men's work seemed utterly ludicrous to most people, she had the courage of her convictions. The War Office, of course, was too dignified to scoff, but its contemptuous indifference was quite as bad. After many hopeless attempts the two friends gave it up and got a job as despatch-riders for the Women's Emergency Corps, which also had the faculty of seeing ahead. Mairi had had no training as a nurse, and was only eighteen, but she had the fundamental qualities of balance, common sense, and loyalty, and so, when the idea of the corps was mooted, Gipsy chose her at once to belong to it. Mairi had no money, but possessed with a burning fervour to help, she sold her beloved motor-cycle to provide the funds for her expenses.

The next selection was a golden-haired American lady, also untrained, but very willing and eager; she turned out to be a beautiful pianist. Miss May Sinclair, the novelist, heard of the project and decided to go too, not as an ambulance helper, but to be useful in any capacity. She offered herself as secretary, and the difficulties she surmounted during her three weeks in Belgium have been ably told in her book *A Journal of Impressions in Belgium*. When the party was thus nearly made up Dr. Munro accepted Lady Dorothie Feilding, whose name became very well known in connection with her work for the corps. The British Red Cross had scoffed at this amateur band, but the Belgian Red Cross was willing enough to accept their useful services; and when the British one found this out it actually rose at length to giving them two cars, which necessitated the addition of two working chauffeurs to the party, and furthermore it eventually gave them their passages to Belgium. Thus when they set out from Victoria for Ostend on that momentous day at the end of September, 1914, the corps had a field of useful work open to them.

There was not one heart among them that was not thrilled as they steamed across the sea amid numerous ships of our own, which gave a cheer when they recognized the Red Cross. All that lay ahead was utterly unknown even to the most experienced of the party, for what likeness does the ordinary healing work in sickness bear to the violent wounds and unnatural smashes of the human body in the grip of war?

Antwerp had not then fallen; the Germans had certainly got a grip on Belgium, but it was not a strangle-hold. The horrible monster was advancing, reaching out with his claws to deal red death to soldier and civilian alike if they lay in his path; and this incomparable little company of gallant people, with a reckless disregard of danger and a divine carelessness as to how they were to be supported, advanced across the water to meet the monster and to rescue from his jaws, it might be, "two legs or a piece of an ear."

★★★★★★

In September, 1913, the crude blues and reds and yellows of the bathing-machines on the yellow *plage* at Ostend had been almost lost amid the still more gaily-hued paddlers and merry-makers who considered that to dip one toe in the water was bathing sufficiently and delightfully. In September, 1914, the bathing-machines were still there, but the crowd was gone. The melancholy-looking crudely painted wooden erections stood up forlornly like huge fungi, and no one used them. Until a day or so before the ambulance corps arrived in Ostend the place had been fairly full, certainly, but with a different crowd from the gay crowd of holiday-makers. No one believed that the Germans would ever get so far as this, but the shadow of the Hun was over the land, rising up ominously on the eastern horizon, and the chill of it cut off the gaiety from a nation which, in one of its sections, was the most pleasure-loving on earth.

Then, only the night before, a message had come from the Germans in the shape of a bomb dropped on the principal hotel adjoining the railway-station. A great exodus of the people occurred at once. The bomb had fallen in the garden and there made a great hole, and one of the first things the party of English people did on arrival was to go out to look at it with awe and excitement a wonderful thing, a hole made by a bomb, the first any of them had seen! Most of them were to gain so much familiarity with shell-holes that they were heartily sickened of them. "Shells, shells, shells!" writes Gipsy in one of her home letters later. "How I wish I could never see them again!"

Except for the hole, it was certainly not much like war-time in Ostend, for the huge hotel, with its luxurious bathrooms provided *en suite* to every bedroom, was still just as usual; but the message that all lights were to be out by 8.30 gave a touch of novelty—it was long before lights had been lowered in England.

The next morning the members of the corps awoke to face a wild scramble and much running to and fro, arising from lack of adequately-thought-out detail.

The party were to go to Ghent, to make their headquarters there for the present. But how were they to get there? There were two cars certainly, one a 42 h.p. Daimler, with pneumatic tyres, for passenger service, and the other a 40 h.p. Fiat, with solid tyres, suitable for carrying baggage. There were the cars and there were the chauffeurs but where was the motive power—the petrol? No one had thought of this, apparently, and at first it was suggested that as petrol seemed unprocurable in Ostend, the cars should be put on a truck and taken by rail to Ghent; but after a weary delay even this was found to be impracticable, for the cars, being very large, refused to go on the trucks. At length, after endless skirmishing up and down and a good deal of irritation, due to pent-up excitement among the members of the party, the military authorities lent them enough petrol to carry them on to Bruges, and about 1.30 they got off, after what seemed an interminable morning, for they had been up by 6.

The road to Bruges runs almost due east, straight into the jaws of that devouring monster which, like the dragon of the old fairy-stories, was scorching up the country-side with his breath. The road, like all the main roads in Belgium, had stones in the middle, the *pavé* sloping down a little at each side, and it was bordered by a ditch and a line of

17

poplar-trees, straight and sentinel-like. There were very few signs of war. Even the guns could not be heard; the ambulance corps motored, as many a hundred parties had motored before them, in perfect serenity; and if it had not been for the sentries whom they had to pass occasionally when passports were demanded, it might have seemed an ordinary holiday. They were all very innocent of what it was they were going to face.

How little did those two bright-eyed girls—for Gipsy herself was little more than a girl—foresee the weeks of cramped quarters, hardly a minute without danger, the horrors of sights and sounds beyond thought, the horrors of want of baths and change of clothes, the horrors of creeping things they had never yet encountered, the icy cold, the continual strain, the rough food and lack of all the refinements of civilization!

As they ran through the villages, little children in wooden clogs and women with apple-red faces or wrinkled nut-brown skins, came out to watch and smile and wave. The very sight of the cars brought hope to them, for were not these British the vanguard of those powerful forces which were coming to save Belgium? Poor souls! They were later to know what German rule meant, with grinding torture when the iron-shod heel of the Hun pressed down upon their daily lives, and screwed as they writhed; for all the goodwill in the world could not manufacture troops in time to stop the Hun before he reached them.

In the generosity of her heart Gipsy showered the cigarettes she had with her on every man she saw; but Mairi, with a characteristic touch, held back hers, knowing that when her friend's ran out and she had no more there would be woe and wailing.

Bruges looked totally undisturbed. The glorious belfry reared itself in all its delicate glory, straight and slender, peeping over the roofs to greet them as the cars thumped over the vile *pavé*. A woman with a little cross-over shawl wrapped round her shoulders was delivering milk from a tiny cart drawn by a patient square-built dog, just as she had done every day for years. The cows must be milked and people must have milk—and there, well, the Germans wouldn't come to Bruges, they would be stopped long before that! It was difficult even for educated people to picture beforehand the destruction and misery which swept like an avalanche on these peaceful towns, and much more so for the uneducated, who had never been anywhere else, and to whom these towns were the world.

Bruges is encircled by a canal, and the cars had to cross it to enter, and then ran on to the Grand Place, pulling up before the Post Office. A Belgian trooper was standing outside, and the untried French of the party was quite sufficient to make him understand that petrol was the chief need; he came to show where it might be bought, and then, with no further delay, out and on they went to Ghent. They were all so incredibly keen to get there, to fling themselves into the red zone of war, to begin to bind up wounds, that the intense stillness of this flat country was almost unendurable.

In the flatness of the calmest sea there is movement and ceaseless stir; the sea is forever whispering some tale to those who have ears to hear. The flatness of the prairie is full of anticipation; no one knows what may not be revealed as each roll of the land is surmounted. The flatness of the desert conceals an infinite mystery, for no human eye, unless it be that of a Bedouin, can sort out into definiteness the shining gradations of lilac and grey and biscuit colour. But all these are as nothing to the flatness of parts of Belgium, which merely waits. And the numb tension of it settled on the hearts of those who were longing for action.

Ghent was reached at about 5.30, and here indeed, everything woke up vividly; about a thousand people were collected in the Grand Place shouting and waving; upper windows were opened and many leaned out; handkerchiefs were flourished, and the cars had to go cautiously in the crowded streets, making a kind of triumphal progress. The whole aspect of the city was as if it had been eagerly awaiting just these two little car-loads of English.

There were two military hospitals in Ghent, and it was to the second, which had received about a hundred wounded men, that the English ambulance was attached. It was really the Flandria Palace Hotel, and the ambulance members were to live there and to have their meals in a great stately room, waited on by two orderlies, Jean and Max, little Belgian soldiers who had been to the front and were convalescing from wounds. No hardship here. For one moment in the evening a thrill of excitement burst out, when the party heard that some of them might be wanted to go out to fetch some wounded, and thus would come in contact with the real thing, and "begin." But it was a false alarm; only one wounded man came in; and he was brought by a horse ambulance. Mairi, indeed, went to see him, thinking in her young zeal she could not begin too soon; she was rewarded by a sight of the bullet which had just been taken from his leg.

The next morning all sorts of tiresome formalities about passports were again necessary, and up and down the crowded streets they passed. Broad clean streets they are—or were—with electric trams running along them, a very different place from sleepy Bruges! Canals run here and there throughout the whole town, cutting it up into slices and chunks, and at almost every street corner there is a view of a quaint bridge and some motionless barges. Down one of the narrow back streets an old woman was sitting by her wooden door; she wore a frilled granny-cap and worked away with heavily knuckled fingers upon a piece of the pillow lace by which she earned her bread. At her feet, jumping endlessly up and down the sunk step of the doorway, was a hideous tiny tortoise-shell kitten, quite pleased with itself and its prospects in life; it would have been hard to say which was the most unmoved by the gathering of the great cataclysm, the kitten of a few weeks, or the old grandmother who had long left behind the romance of her life. Possibly her grandsons were now among the hundreds of sturdily built, ruddy-cheeked young men who faced the terrific blasts of the German artillery.

In the Béguinage de Mont St. Armand lived nuns, in immense flapping white headgear. For years they had been within those sheltering walls, praying and fasting and doing a little lace-making, and now they were soon to be suddenly thrust into a world running red with blood, with every vestige of the curtain concealing the fierce realities of life torn away. Not far from their wall, which was still intact and seemed to radiate something of the somnolence from within, as bricks radiate the heat when the sun has passed on, stood a German car, captured and brought in by the great armoured car that stood beside—it a conscious conqueror. The German car shrieked of the force that had been used in its destruction, which had riddled its radiator with holes, smashed its screen to powder, and crushed its vital power. Across the twisted steering-wheel were smears of half-dried blood, and wavering over the driving-seat hung a torn and ghastly rag.

The next two days were dreadfully trying to Gipsy Knocker and Mairi Chisholm, for here they were "on the spot," but, as they phrased it, "nothing doing." They could not help in nursing the wounded, for there were plenty of nurses—besides, that was not their job; their part was to go out to the firing-line to fetch the wounded and render first-aid, and bring them in, but no one had sent for them and they had no permission to go.

They visited the refugees who had come in from the country-side,

A Backwater.

The Staple House, Ghent

escaping from under the fringe of the great cloud that rolled ever westward. There were as many as eight thousand at that time in Ghent, and they had been housed, by a strange irony, in the Palais des Fêtes! Straw had been heaped up round some of the halls, and here they lay, whole families together, robbed by shock of all power of initiative, stunned by the earthquake that had flung them up and out of the places where they had lived their simple lives. All links with the past, every treasured household remembrance, had been wrenched from them, and the future was an utter blank. Something of that bewilderment, amounting to agony, which overtakes one occasionally when one awakes after a deep dream and cannot regain the everyday self was theirs in terrible measure. In the spacious storey above mothers were even now bringing forth babies, with no country, no place in the world, no prospects.

The feeding of all these people was an enormous task, and it is to the credit of Ghent that it was so well tackled. Some of the ambulance party helped, cutting up huge chunks of bread, setting out bowls of soup, and working till their backs ached, on the principle of doing anything that might be useful; but even this was denied them, for they were recalled by authority, for fear they might carry germs to the wounded when they handled them.

CHAPTER 2

In the Thick of a Battle

By September 29, three days after they had arrived in Ghent, Gipsy's vital energy had got too much for her, and she had to do something or explode; so she found a job in driving the car of the Belgian Colonel, whose own chauffeur had disappeared. She fell into this niche, which fitted her to a nicety, in the simplest and most feminine way possible, because she walked up to look at the Belgian trenches outside the town, and found the colonel minus a coat button. Of course she sewed it on, and followed up the obvious opening by offering to fill the place as chauffeur. Though the Belgian Army was not nearly so much swathed about with red tape as some of the older countries, yet it was rather an innovation that the colonel should accept a woman as chauffeur in war-time, and therefore certain formalities had to be faced. These were got through with the speed born of necessity, and the following day Gipsy took the colonel on his rounds to various outposts, picking up a wounded man on the way. She had coffee with her new employer before he went on to the actual front, and she concluded that he was "a dear, so kind and considerate;" he had not taken any advantage of the unusual position.

Already it was beginning to be apparent that there was a fatal lack of organization in the ambulance corps. The men part of it were rushing hither and thither bravely enough, but in a most haphazard manner, wasting much precious petrol, and even joy-rides were not unknown, whereas much real ability and energy was running to waste.

Various signs of military activity were to be seen through Ghent from time to time. Some field-guns caused a diversion, and when numbers of sturdy plucky Belgian troops marched through, the lady members of the corps gave them cigarettes to express that sympathy which for the moment they seemed to have no other way of expressing.

The post of chauffeur, after all, took up very little time, and even this outlet was blocked, for Dr. Munro, rather naturally, objected to one of his corps being taken off for such work, and it had to be stopped. Gipsy and Mairi therefore amused themselves playing games with the convalescent soldiers, but all the while brain and heart were under a terrific strain; there is no strain quite so bad as waiting in the certainty that any moment you may be called upon to put forth all your resources and face scenes so horrible that you may fail, for even the best of us never knows his calibre until tried. "We mouched around," says Mairi miserably. "I felt bored with life. Another day of waiting! One must have patience beyond everything!" Then there swam into their ken the gay and gallant figure of a young Belgian officer; he was slim and tall, with fair hair, showing up in contrast with his well-fitting dark green uniform. They nicknamed him "Gilbert the Filbert." At that time he was with the Voluntary Cyclists Corps, and used to go out at nights on his motor-cycle to pick off German outposts; he had accounted for forty-eight Germans in the weeks preceding, so his presence was inspiriting. He was to be very closely associated with them in their work, but at the time he was merely a passer-by.

The first serious work came when the trainloads of wounded men had to be met at the station at any hour of the night, and conveyed to the hospitals. In the dark and icy-cold station the friends waited hour after hour for the trains which never came when they were expected. They snatched hurried moments trying to rest in a rail-way carriage, but the cold was so intense that sleep was out of the question. Sometimes they talked to the men in charge of the solid, heart-cheering British omnibuses, straight from London, having their shiny sides painted with Clapham, Cricklewood, and other names which seemed more lovable and attractive than London suburbs ever did before. There was a dramatic moment when a trainload of terribly smashed and maimed Belgians came in at one platform of the station, just as a trainload of self-confident, clean, fresh British Tommies was going out from another.

The little Belgians had not as yet seen such assurances of help, and one and all, exhausted and faint as they were, cheered and waved their poor bandaged hands; while, as the other train began to move, the Tommies looked at them in pleased shyness, not in the least knowing how to show they appreciated the welcome. "Give them a cheer, boys!" shouted Gipsy, letting loose the spring at the psychological moment, and the resounding shout in response echoed through the vaults of the gloomy station roof.

The girls worked with the strength of ten; when none of the men of the party were available they even did the heavy lifting, raising the dead weight of unconscious or helpless men on stretchers. They worked sometimes right through the night, so that when they got back to their quarters in the morning there was only time to wash and be ready again for what the day should bring forth, for they might be wanted at any moment. "I never felt so googly and utterly played out in my life," says Mairi after one such night. Still, they had comfortable rooms to go back to, and good food when they wanted it; this was child's-play to what came afterwards. The waiting, which had seemed so interminable to their eager hearts strung up to expectation, really endured for only a few days, and they soon began to range around the outlying villages to find wounded men.

By the beginning of October they had learnt many things. They had seen the Belgians working busily at digging trenches, in absolute silence, so as not to attract the Germans, who were only a hundred yards away. They had run along in the open, expecting any moment to be noticed and made a target for shells. They had had the most discouraging of all experiences, that of seeing their allies obliged to retreat. In one place they passed through one of those experiences which remain like a hurt on the heart. Fifty men had been left to guard the retreat of the rest, left to what was almost certain death. Theirs to hold up the flood-tide so long as they might before going under. There was a look on the faces of these men seen only on the faces of the dead who have died in peace. There was no uncertainty, no disquietude. They awaited their fate as if they had already met it, not lightly or discounting what it meant, but with the calm willing-ness of those who had seen all they loved in the world swept away. The clear blue eyes of every rough soldier had in them something of the light that comes from a vision of the beyond. There was no faltering, but no braggart conceit; they were invincible alive or dead.

And the fate that descended on them was not left only to the imagination of those who perhaps might have found it difficult to imagine, having had no previous experience of such things. For a few days later Gipsy, going out with some of the men of the ambulance, came upon what was left of just such another group, at Nazareth, not far from Zele. Twenty-six military police holding an outpost had been surrounded by about three hundred Germans, who had acted accord-

THE MEN WHO WORKED THE GUNS

THE FLATNESS OF BELGIUM

ONE OF THE INNUMERABLE CANALS.

ing to their kind and passed on.

The Belgians had resisted to the death, and the whole twenty-six lay there, pitched about in various attitudes. They had been shot at by a ring of their foes at a range of from ten to fifteen yards, but that was not all. Even this finished slaughter had not satiated the Germans' stomach for blood, and they had deliberately set to work to mutilate and rob the dead foe. That tiny plot of grass was rusty with blood. Every face was smashed in except that of the captain, who had been shot through the heart and left as he was, to be identified, possibly with the cool intention of showing that the leader had not escaped. From the others everything had been stolen—boots, purses, stockings, and other clothes—so that the dead were nearly naked, and even their identification discs had been removed.

One of the first times Gipsy and Mairi were actually under fire was on October 5, and it was at Berleare, a little village about four miles west of Termonde and a good way east of Ghent. The account is best told in Gipsy's own simple wording, taken from one of her letters home, which was afterwards reproduced in a local paper:

We went through busy lines of cavalry, and all the way along the firing got louder and louder. We ran into Berleare about 9.30 a.m., and about 9.45 a big shell fell on a neighbouring house and shattered the roof. I was able to get a large piece. While we were standing listening to the fearful noise of shell and rifle fire, the order came through that there were wounded at Appels to be fetched. Off we went, and we found that we were bound to leave the ambulance close to the main road and walk with the stretchers, as we had to go toward the river, and the Germans were the other side. We had to walk about three miles, and then came to the river (Dendre).

The river was, I suppose, about fifty yards wide, with a high trench built on either side. We had to creep, bent double, all along the side, until we came to these wounded men. I will try and explain the position. The river bank had been highly trenched, and there was a pathway along the side of the trench, about five yards wide. There was a steep bank descent, and at the bottom a boggy water-meadow country, with only a small foot pathway, raised out of the water, across each field. At 2 p.m. it began to rain heavily, and it was difficult keeping one's feet on the muddy, wet ground, as it was thought safer to walk on the bottom of the bank in the water.

So our little band trudged on with four damp stretchers and our heavy box of dressings. At last, lying on the soaking grass and wet through, we discovered a Belgian Tommy almost exhausted and terribly wounded; his right foot carried away by shrapnel and also shot badly in the back. We did what we could for him, but we could only put him on a damp stretcher and leave him in charge of someone while we went on. No talking was allowed, as sounds carry over the river. All this time the shells were whizzing over our heads and rifle-fire was heard all round.

We crept along the bank, slipping and falling, until we saw on the river pathway, just behind the trench, the uniform of a Belgian Major. He was badly shot in the thigh, and had to be carefully attended. It was terribly difficult work, as the German patrol spotted us on the other side of the river, and it was not a pleasant moment. If you can imagine us exactly between the two firing-lines, you have some idea of our position. You can imagine those big shells whizzing over our heads, and with lives to save, it was not a moment to laugh. We had to carry the major practically along the ground—that is, we had to be bent nearly double, so that our heads were below the level of the river trench. I wonder if anyone can realize what it means. I only ask them to put a heavy grown man on a stretcher and attempt to carry him by bending double; it is a terribly difficult and exhausting proceeding, and all the time that awful heavy fire. And it was getting so dark that it was hard to see. Suddenly everything was lit up by the firing of some houses in Berleare by the Germans.

We nearly got lost on the way home. We had to tramp over the fields those three miles back to rejoin the ambulances, resting every fifty yards to change arms and bearers. I shall never forget the evening. We could not light a match on account of being watched by the Germans. But we managed to find our ambulance and get the men home at last. How plucky these little Belgians are!

To this account it may be added that the danger of getting back to Berleare was much emphasized by the great dykes full of water to be crossed somehow, and that the cheeriness of the whole expedition was enhanced by a steady downpour of rain.

One day came the news that Antwerp had been evacuated. Even if they had not heard it they would have known it by the flood of fugitives which poured into Ghent. The roads were choked by them, men and women and children, piled on carts or dragging hand-barrows, some, who had lost all they loved—children, husbands, wives, or mothers, without much prospect of ever again discovering them— were still clinging grimly and quite unconsciously to a tawdry ornament or some such trifle, snatched up automatically and gripped with the grip that death does not loosen.

Out of all this welter of horror one or two scenes stand out by reason of the pathetic touch. An old woman of the working classes was conveying a small cart dragged by a dog; in the cart sat two wee babes, probably her grandchildren. The dog had been wounded, for his fore-paw was bleeding, and he limped along painfully, but with great determination and full consciousness of his immense responsibility. Every now and then he turned his brown eyes on his mistress, as if asking permission, and then sank down on the roadside to lick his paw, while the stream of amazingly mixed traffic swept by on each side of him. The old granny looked at him mutely, but did not hurry him; she knew that in him lay the sole chance of her babies reaching safety, for she was too old and weak to carry them. If the dog failed they would die, and therefore she waited with feeble resignation until he himself, without being urged, took up the collar-work of his little living load and staggered on.

It was the sense of personal isolation which struck one most in these crowds. In normal life if one falls out by the way there are always any number of healthy and well-to-do folk to give a hand; but here, where each tiny group was tried to the utmost in struggling up out of their own avalanches of misfortune, there was no one who, however willing, could help. It was sink or swim for each family or individual, alone.

Most of the people in this crowd were Flemings, and they are a curious race. Nothing seems to disturb them. As they tramped along in hundreds it was rare to see a woman in tears. They seemed to accept the inevitable with a stoical patience; no questions were asked, no complaints made, and there was certainly not the least sign of panic. They trudged along, scarcely paying any attention to the troops they met, or those that passed them marching, also in retreat. Their absolute lack of emotion was almost uncanny; their faces were unnaturally calm. To an outsider it appeared as if it might be the calm of unintelligence, but the look of pain in the eyes of some of them contradicted that theory. The Two could not help asking, "What lies behind that mask of indifference? Are there any feelings there at all?" It is difficult for one of another race to understand the Flamand. Is he only stupid, or is there a lack of frankness in his nature which forbids one to trust him entirely? Most of these people were agriculturists—the Flamand does not take kindly to mechanical work. These strong, thick-set men and women looked what they were, farm-labourers born and bred, without any streak of the vivacity of their fellow-countrymen the Walloons.

One day a message was brought to the ambulance corps that there was a wounded officer awaiting rescue in a shattered house at Lokeren, then on the very furthest fringe of the Belgian territory, up against the German lines. On the way out indeed, the ambulance in which Gipsy was, passed part of the Belgian Army in retreat. But this did not deter the party; on they went past those stained and worn men who were still unconquered and as resolute in retreat as in advance. Some of the last of them stopped a minute and pointed out the house where the wounded man was to be found, before they hurried after their comrades, and were lost in that dull-coloured mass of muddy clothes and torn uniforms.

The place was a little cottage, which had received some battering, but was still comparatively whole; it looked utterly deserted. With tense expectation the rescuers pushed open the door, and stopped for a moment to get used to the gloom; there was a horribly eerie sound ringing through the emptiness, a drip, drip, steady and unexplained, like the drip of a kitchen tap. Then the cause was revealed, for on the table lay an officer, a young man in the prime of life, in a beautiful new uniform with brightly polished buttons and stars gleaming, and as he lay there his blood dropped slowly and steadily on to the floor, draining away his life. He was beyond help.

As the party left the house the German forces poured in at the other end of the village.

However, the ambulances had already picked up three other wounded soldiers, and they felt their perilous dash into danger had been worthwhile. When they were almost clear of the houses on the way back a blind man came slowly groping towards them, and they stopped for him, though they knew that the Germans were right behind them. He advanced, but his movements were slow, and he had only placed one foot on the step when a burst of rifle-fire told them that they were fully in range, and were being deliberately made a target of. It was a choice between the life of one civilian and three wounded soldiers, and they decided for the latter, and went off at full speed. It is, however, satisfactory to hear that the blind man was afterwards brought in safely by an armoured car.

The party had hardly returned to Ghent when a call came for them to go to Melle, a little village about six miles off on the main road running south-east from Ghent. Here the Two were to have one of the greatest experiences of their lives—one of those experiences which scores a deep mark across consciousness, so that the "after" can never again be quite as the "before."

When they arrived at Melle at about 8 o'clock at night they were told by soldiers who were dodging round the houses that the main street was "cleared for action," and that they must on no account go there; so the ambulance was drawn up in a side-street right in the heart of the battle, for close behind it was the Belgian artillery. Wounded men soon began to require aid, and the car was quickly filled and ran back to Ghent, to return again just as the Germans made a rush and swept down the main street. Unimaginable uproar and confusion resulted. Shells were not actually bursting in the town, because neither side could be sure of not hitting their own men, but the artillery were hard at work sky-rocketing their missiles at one another overhead to prevent reinforcements coming up, and in among the houses a perfect storm of bullets hissed like deadly hail, rebounding off the houses or lodging in the crevices of the woodwork. It cannot have been given to many women, especially those of another race than the combatants, to have been in the thick of such a battle.

The French marines were helping the Belgians, and both together were resisting in a desperate fight, the most deadly fighting of all, hand-to-hand combats hemmed in by houses. It was quite dark, for there was no moon, and all around the ambulance party were little groups of French marines awaiting the word of command to spring into action. Some of them brought up a stretcher, whispering about the *blessé* who was on it, hit in the leg. Groping to feel the horrible wound, Gipsy leant over him and began bandaging, and then some inertness made her aware she could do nothing. At her request a match was struck, and she saw her surmise was true, the man was already dead.

Then there were sudden shouts and the jangle of field equipment and a hideous scuffle, and all in the dark, right around the car, Belgians and French and Germans inextricably mixed in bayonet-fighting swept past. The car held already one badly wounded man, and it was about time to move, so when the tense moment was past they worked their way out of the town to go back. But in doing so they naturally came under shell-fire, and hardly had they started than shells burst within fifty yards of them, crashing into the ground and exploding with volumes of sickening smoke, leaving great pits.

It was mere touch-and-go whether one would not land on the top of the ambulance and exterminate the whole party, but they escaped injury as by a miracle, and arriving at the hospital, left their precious burden and actually returned once more through the deadly fire-zone. The scene had changed; the combined Belgians and French had thrust back the invaders, and the town was saved, the line being where it had been before. Perhaps the most remarkable feature of the whole episode was the coolness of Mairi. This girl of eighteen, who had so little experience to prepare her, had been under fire the whole afternoon and through this awful turmoil; and in her diary, written with no intention of anyone ever seeing it, but merely as a personal record, she writes:

It was most interesting; the shrapnel was screaming overhead the whole time—a most fascinating sound.

Gipsy's comment is:

We got more than we wanted: we nearly lost the ambulance. Mairi and I were on the step under heavy fire, and I saw a German soldier with a good eye taking deliberate aim at us.

One *would* feel instinctively that he had a good eye!

She too, ends up on a note of exultation:

It was a wonderful and grand day, and I would not have missed it for anything.

Chapter 3

The Field of Mercy

In the midst of this whirlpool of madness and misery Melle was inhabited. There were old men and women and children whose homes were in those shot-torn houses, and they had cowered there while the shells hurtled overhead and the piercing bullets flew like arrows. After this fearful day there were a larger number of wounded civilians than usual. The nuns at the convent had their hands quite full. The dull dreamy current of their lives had dashed into a vortex, and in it they had had to stretch out hands of help and pity to those who were drowning beside them. As Gipsy came into the convent next morning, she was overwhelmed with pity at the spectacle of the wounded people there.

Somehow it is so much worse to see civilians wounded than soldiers; soldiers, at all events, know what they are out for, but these poor—sheep She stepped over to one little girl of about eight, who was horribly torn in the stomach and lay gazing wide-eyed at Fear. At least that was what the expression in her eyes conveyed; she seemed to have seen "Fear "large and personified in front of her, and was unable to wrench her gaze from the grisly spectre. As Gipsy drew near she started and tried to pull away her hand with a little terrified moan, but after a moment nestled nearer to her, as if she wanted to shut out that awful sight that was burnt in all the while in her own poor brain. The village was a village of horrors; the dead were piled up in hundreds, friend and foe together, and there was no time to bury them while the danger was so imminent.

It was known that there must be lying around the town at no great distance hundreds of wounded and maimed, longing for aid, and desperate measures must be taken to get at them and shepherd them in. Gipsy and Mairi Chisholm, whose friendship had been cemented by the ghastly night, so that it was firmer than ever, walked out alone across three fields in the direction of the hottest fighting, and they climbed off the road to what looked like a peaceful turnip-field; and not until they reached it did they notice that among the turnips were many curious grey humps, and with a sudden thrill realized that here were the dead and the dying they had come to seek. Some doctors, in fact, were already at work crouching down, and seeing them, called out to them to come and help. Most of the bodies were in that cold grey-green uniform the colour of which seemed some-how to have got into the air and sky, and tinted them a cold grey-green too—a colour which will forever after be associated in the mind of every Belgian with horrors unspeakable.

The very first man they saw lying by the hedge was stone-dead, shot through the jaw. Another not far off lay on his back, his face a bloody mask upturned to the frowning sky; he was still as marble, except for his right knee, which twitched regularly, ceaselessly, like a returning pulse. Gipsy hastened over to the help of the doctor who had called her, as Mairi fell on her knees beside this man, and at that moment, without warning or expectation, a salvo of German shells burst around them. They had been observed in their work of mercy and were being shot at! "Catch them, wipe them out! Good job too! Why bother with the wounded—our own or the others? What use is a wounded man anymore? Let them die!" Thus spoke the batteries, and the shells fell faster.

If the wounded had been Belgians or French, it is probable that the devoted workers would not have left them even then; but to be fired at by Germans while succouring Germans was rather too much, and they fled for the time.

But the thought of those wretched wounded men, with broken and smashed bone and muscle, agonizing in thirst, their life-blood draining into the broad-leaved turnips, pulled at the warm hearts of the men and women from England, and once again later they tried to get at them. They took the ambulance, and left it at the nearest point on the road, and went off again across that stretch of field where dead cows with grotesquely inflated bodies lay in the corners. When they reached the turnip-field, they found some pigs rootling among those dead heaps of clothing, a sight that turned them sick for all their courage; but they went on, and had hardly gained their field of mercy, hardly had time to note that the awful pulsing movement of that right knee was still ceaselessly continuing without cessation or rest, when the guns were burst upon them again, and they had to withdraw once more.

They still stayed in the town, in the hope that somehow after dark they might reach that field of death and carry out a rescue. During the afternoon a car came in to Melle with three dead German officers and a chauffeur who had escaped with his life by the merest fraction. They had driven too near the Belgian lines, and three of the four had been wiped out by the Belgian armoured car.

When dusk fell at last Gipsy and Mairi made an urgent request to Dr. Munro that they might be allowed to go back to the turnip-field, for they would have risked their lives indifferently for friend or foe, so long as they were wounded and helpless. Dr. Munro, however, quite rightly refused. They had been twice driven off by the fire of the Germans—why jeopardize valuable lives and the precious ambulance? As they discussed the question a Belgian Red Cross car ran into the village, and the Two eagerly applied to the doctor in charge to help them. He could not resist their earnest pleading, and carried them along with him to the field.

It was almost dark when they worked softly into position as near to the scene of action as possible, and then stepped gently down, and thrusting aside the *osier* bushes that line the road, crept, holding their breath, out to those awfully still humped grey forms. They reached the man that the doctor and Gipsy had begun to bandage that day, but he was already dead, killed by the brutality of his own comrades when he might have had a chance of life. Then they instinctively drew nearer to each other as they glanced toward that other silent form, and there, regularly as the second-hand of a clock, that awful galvanic movement went on, as it had done for hour after hour: the twitching of the right knee up and down, up and down! They picked up the poor wretch, who seemed quite unconscious, on a stretcher and carried him back to the ambulance, but he died the same night.

When the wounded had been safely transferred to cars to go back to Ghent, yet once again the two women went out with the Belgian military doctor, past the French outposts, and waited there for him under a railway bridge while he and another man went off to reconnoitre. It was all so still it might have been the day after death and before resurrection, as indeed it was for many. A tense dead stillness surrounded them, hanging heavily on ears vibrating still with the hellish scream of the shells. There was no moon, but a kind of diffused greyness which conveyed a curious idea that it might any moment burst into brilliant and unearthly light.

The car went back to Melle and then to Ghent, and there Gipsy, hearing that someone was needed at Melle all night, went yet again back in it, leaving Mairi to go to bed. But hardly had Mairi been in bed an hour, and fallen asleep with the heavy overpowering sleep of a child, than a light flashed in her eyes and she was told to get up, as all the ambulances had been called out. No wonder each day seemed as if it had been a month! She went out in the big Daimler car with two of the men of the party, and half-way to Melle the big car bumped wildly and danced off the *pavé* into the mud; a tyre was punctured! When everyone is dog-tired such incidents are bound to happen, but despair is a word unknown to members of ambulance corps of the right sort.

By great good luck another car came cautiously along in the dark, almost tumbling on the top of the first. It belonged to a Belgian doctor, who picked up the little Scottish girl and carried her on to Melle. Here she was greeted by her friend, white and worn, but quite cheery, and heard it was a false alarm, for after all they were not needed! So back they went to the Flandria in the same car, landing there about four in the morning.

No wonder Melle is written ineffaceably on their minds! It was here that they first saw the dead and wounded in masses. Here they found themselves in the thick of an actual battle. It was the chief centre of their activities in those days at Ghent, the village they saw first and last, and the name will always stand out in letters of flame.

CHAPTER 4

The Retreat

But Ghent did not long remain a refuge; well before the middle of the month earnest warnings to evacuate it were given. The way in which the final summons came was dramatic. Mairi was in bed, sleeping with her usual heart-whole earnestness, when she was awakened suddenly, and saw standing by her one of the doctors attached to the ambulance, telling her the Germans were upon them and they must fly. Then followed a scramble. The first thing was to save the wounded soldiers, who must not be left to fall into the hands of the foe. Alas! the order had come through the day before that all the kits belonging to these men were to be sent to Ostend as a measure of precaution.

One of those "decisions in blinkers" which cause such infinite suffering. The patients were mostly in thin cotton pyjamas; the night was foggy and bitterly cold; the only conveyance was an open transport waggon with a scanty layer of straw on the boards. Gipsy and Mairi rummaged for all the blankets they could find, and wrapped the poor fellows up in them; but it must have been a terrible journey for many of them. They were drawn by horses, and could only go at a walking pace on account of the direful roads, the quantity of traffic already occupying them, and the darkness of the night. And they had to cover fifty miles to gain safety! When they were finally sent off the members of the corps had to think of themselves.

There was none too much room in the cars, and they had to pack in like sardines. As Gipsy had been sitting up with a wounded officer when the summons came, and since then, having been occupied with the soldiers, had not been able to change the cotton hospital dress she happened to be wearing, she suffered frightfully from the cold. The cars crawled along to Eccloo, where they stopped at the house of an Englishwoman, a friend of Dr. Munro's. Although this lady and her husband were themselves preparing to fly, they received the rather forlorn party with the utmost kindness, and spread abundance of blankets on the floor of the drawing-room, where they made up a roaring fire. There they all waited till daybreak. A strangely assorted party they were, lying about in all directions, some on the window-seats, some on the floor, and the two chauffeurs betrayed their qualifications by falling sound asleep with their mouths open, sitting bolt upright on two stiff-backed chairs, a feat that filled some of the others with admiration.

After breakfast next morning they all followed the wounded, and reached Bruges in time to get them into the convent hospital by midday. The stiff cold men had been unpacked, and fed, and laid in comfortable beds, and were beginning to recover a little from their awful night, when like a thunderbolt came the news that the Germans had entered Ghent at seven that morning, and that twelve thousand of them, ruthless men, without pity or consideration for the fallen, were hastening forward to Bruges; so all the poor tired soldiers had to be carried down again, and sent onward once more. It was heart-rending work.

This time the objective was Ostend, and along that poplar-lined road, which had seemed so peaceful when they ran the other way in high hopes about three weeks ago, back the Munro ambulance people went with heavy hearts. The nearer they drew to Ostend, the greater grew the crush. It seemed as if the whole population of Belgium must be converging on the port, the last link of the chain which England held. Hospital ambulances, troops, refugees, guns, transport, carts, were surging together and every now and then jammed. There was much cursing and swearing in a variety of tongues. In the town, streets, shops, houses, were packed with people; it seemed as if they must all be welded into a jelly, and unable to extricate themselves until the Germans arrived. The mental harassment of seeing to the wounded added tenfold to the strain on those responsible, and the relief was great when, at last, they were got on to a boat going across to England, which carried no less than seven thousand wounded men!

With the lifting of this terrible load the personal troubles of the ambulance were by no means ended, only now they had time to think of themselves. So desperate was the situation considered that no baggage was allowed to be taken off the cars. Still in her cotton dress, now soiled and crushed in a way to depress the heart of the most careless of women, Gipsy had to pass another night; and all night long

The French come to help

Engineer's cart smashed by a shell

FURNES

consciousness was beating at the back of her half-awake brain that any moment the summons to continue the weary flight might sound. Rumours flew fast. The advance of the Germans was at a terrible pace. They would be here before morning! Already they were here! Their numbers swelled to hundreds of thousands—all was over! Though the worst of these forebodings proved untrue, yet the situation was bad enough. The work seemed smashed across the middle, past possibility of recovery, and there was a horrid knell of defeat to deaden and depress energies already heavily overtaxed.

That evening in Ostend, Mairi came across an elderly man in civilian clothes, much too small for him, standing at a street-corner, with tears running down his cheeks. She remembered having noticed him a few hours earlier in a *garde civique* uniform, and greeting him in the informal way that necessity teaches, she learnt his tale of woe. It was poured out on her in a flood of mingled French and Flemish, in that half-whimsical, half-serious way that told her he was sorely hurt; and as her French had already improved, she gathered the gist of it even before she was helped out by a Cockney Tommy who stood beside him.

> 'E sys, lydy, that orders is froo for 'em to put off of them clothes; he ain't a soldier, and them Boches, if they cetch 'im, why, they'll 'eng him in 'em. I seen 'im done it. 'E's pitched 'em in the sea, all them noo clothes. Gord! I wish I had had 'em on a Sunday morning in the East End! I'd 'ev got more'n a quid for 'em! 'E's right-down sore, 'e is, pore old blighter! And thet's what 'tis all about. Na, I not speak his lingo—for why? 'Tain't necessary; I can understand these chaps wifout, and that's for why.

Mairi left them with a mingled feeling of laughing and crying; it seemed so preposterous that the great stout citizen who had given up his spare time and trained in peace should now have this awful humiliation forced upon him, the knowledge that he was only a play-soldier and no use at all. To be held in disdain; to be forced, by his own action in throwing away his beloved uniform, to confess it was all make-believe and no use when real war came this was worse than being wounded. And there were hundreds of his kind doing the same thing. In Ghent the canals were choked with the heavy coats and belts flung away at the fierce threat of a shameful and ignominious end. It seemed, after all, as if the plight of the *Gardes Civiques* was more pitiable than that of the ambulance corps.

By nine the next morning a greatly swelled procession was marshalled out of the town on the road to Dunkirk; everyone had to keep in position and go at one pace, which was necessarily a crawl. There were about three hundred and fifty cars in the line, including those of two Belgian Generals and others belonging to Ministers. Most depressing of all was the news—which turned out after all to be untrue—that the Diplomats accredited to Belgium had gone to England. That horrible morning left its mark on the Two. Each hour, spun to extremity by the tension within, had upon them the effect of three in power of exhaustion, and yet they really got to Dunkirk not much after midday. Here again was the inextricable confusion, the crush and push. In contemplating war one looks at it usually in the light of history, when events are clear-cut and told with precision. Of the horrible uncertainties, the dubious outlook, the impossibility of reliable information, the difficulty of correct judgment on the spot, only those who are in the midst of it are aware.

Even at Dunkirk there was no room; men were sleeping on the billiard-tables in the hotels. So the two friends went out to a little bathing-place on the coast called Malo-les-Bains. But they were now in Belgium no longer, and the feeling that they had been forced to leave the country they had come to help weighed heavily on them.

"I think I never felt so truly miserable," says Gipsy, "as the moment when we passed the frontier line between Belgium and France. I have left my heart behind me in that brave, honest little country. I shall always think of Belgium as the first country in the world for bravery, honesty, chivalry, and patriotism, and it will be my fervent prayer that they may someday get their country back again. There is something about Belgium that no other country has. I think my heart will always feel more Belgian than British in future"—which embodied an unconscious prophecy.

It was probably the first time Malo-les-Bains had ever had any visitors so late in October, and it must have been puzzled and overwhelmed by this strange honour. Inexpressibly dreary was Malo, with its long level *plage* and straight sea-line, seen through a curtain of steadily pouring rain. The rows of empty bathing-sheds faced the sea like sentry-boxes, and the little, cold, inadequate fringes of foam crept hesitatingly to their doors as if they hardly knew what to make of it all. There were still a few fishing-boats about, and a few men shrimping, mostly very old men, who "must eat." The whole of this place was transformed by war, and the overflow from Dunkirk more than sufficed to overcrowd it as it had never been overcrowded in its gayest season. It was here that the party were joined by the authoress, the late Miss Macnaughtan, who afterwards established a soup-kitchen in Furnes, and did excellent work there at the railway-station among the hungry and bewildered soldiers.

Malo was crammed with troops. There were the British with the strong unmistakable Manchester accent of self-confidence; the French in their heavy and clumsy-looking overcoats; Senegalese shivering arid wilted by a climate which spoilt the delightful game of war; and, of course, plenty of Belgians. Now and again a Taube hovered overhead, fiercely hawk-like, and got well shot at; and once a British aeroplane descended hurriedly, emitting sulphurous language, because it had been unrecognized and included in the too cordial welcome. At night all lights were out save the great searchlights which, like the Flaming Swords of the Angel of Eden, pierced the flatness of the forsaken sands.

On October 20 began what resulted in the tremendous fight for Ypres, when the Germans were thrust back, and those who had thought Belgium all lost took heart again. The mixed population on the coast thinned down again. Those who had given up heart went on further into France, the soldiers were moved, the refugees absorbed else-where. The place in these circumstances looked more dreary than ever, and, to add to their woes, the friends had a personal grief.

Gilbert was missing—Gilbert, who had so endeared himself to the corps that they felt for him as for a lifelong friend. They had seen nothing of him after the hasty summons to leave Ghent, and they greatly feared he had fallen, and was lost in the great swathes of the nameless and unburied. Dr. Munro had gone over to England to get help to start the work anew, and Mairi and Gipsy spent the few uncertain days at Malo wandering about, walking into Dunkirk on the pretence of shopping, and trying to make the best of the contradictory news that filtered in.

One day they suddenly saw a familiar green uniform on a straight, slim young figure, with the head held proudly and lightly as ever. There was no mistaking that gait and that gay insouciance; even before they had caught a glimpse of his face they had flown toward him with outstretched hands. Gilbert laughed and seemed pleased at their solicitude. Oh, he was all right. He had stayed with his regiment to hold up the German vanguard and allow time for the evacuation of Ghent; but he had got off all right, scot-free, not even a wound. "You

45

won't have the pleasure of nursing me; I believe you're really disappointed," he chaffed in his quick French, and Mairi's shrewd eyes saw the tender, quizzical look he gave her friend. Instantly it darted into her mind that there was something behind all this. Gipsy's white face and worried, preoccupied manner had not been only for a surface friend. Mairi was clever beyond her years, and a loyal little soul; she led the way to the sea-shore, indicating the road back to Malo, and then quietly absented herself, and they did not miss her!

As she turned rather sadly by herself to go back into the town she was hailed by one of the British naval officers she knew. He caught sight of her at once, for the streets were comparatively empty; every kind of vehicle had been requisitioned for the flight. There was a hideous, dead-alive look settling down on Dunkirk.

"Come along and have a joy-ride in the last taxi-cab left in Dunkirk," he cried out cheerily. "An experience to record!" She assented readily, feeling rather lost without her almost inseparable companion. Her mind, indeed, was busily at work as she sat there beside this clean frank boy, who looked like a Spaniard, so dark was his colouring. Of course, it was inevitable that Gipsy would marry again some time. She was so good-looking, so high-spirited, so charming, that many, many men would want to marry her; and oh, she did so love to be loved! Therein lay the danger! Was Gilbert good enough? After all, they knew very little about him. He was attractive enough personally, but he was not of their race. Mairi would, of course, never spoil sport; if Gipsy was glad to walk alone with him, walk alone with him she should! If she wanted to marry him, marry him she must; only *she* could decide. But then she was impulsive, her enthusiasm could be caught at the high tide, and what if such a match were not for her happiness? In some ways Mairi often felt older than her friend. "The dear kid!" she said half aloud.

"The blue eyes are very clouded today," remarked Lieutenant N——, turning his own black ones on his companion.

He said it very nicely and not offensively, but Mairi sat up, on her dignity at once. That sort of thing was all right for Gipsy, who had been married already and could put up with it; but as for her, she had other things to do than marry—at present, at all events. In the far future, of course, it would be all right, but when it came in her case it would be a very serious, forever-and-a-day business.

"Do you believe in mixed marriages?" she asked, refusing to respond to the personality.

MRS. KNOCKER IN HER MERCEDES CAR.

A POSTE DE SECOURS.

MRS. KNOCKER ON THE SAND-DUNES.

DR. VAN DER GHINST INTRODUCES HIMSELF TO
MAIRI CHISHOLM.

"Depends what sort of 'mixed,'" the naval man replied briskly, making an opening for himself out of the most unpromising material, as is the way of the navy. "Old and young? Rich and poor? Fair and dark? Land and sea?" The last two very significantly, bending his own close-cropped, dark head down toward the girl's fair hair. "I believe in the last two all the time!"

Mairi looked at him quite candidly and fearlessly, without a trace of *coquetry*. "I haven't any use for that sort of thing," she announced simply; "I'm a Scot," and she wondered why he laughed so merrily.

Dr. Munro returned next day with the news that all was well, and that they were to have headquarters at Furnes, in Belgium, and continue the work. The party was to be reorganized, and M. de Broqueville, one of the sons of the Belgian War Minister, was to command one division of it. This was a great help, as naturally, with all the goodwill in the world, an ambulance party, which has to go into the most secret places and which can't help poking into matters that must be kept secret, is on delicate ground when run entirely by another race, even though they be the closest of allies. This addition would put them on an unassailable footing. The British Field Hospital was also to be re-established at Furnes and work in connection with the corps.

Gilbert also was to be attached to the party, and was to drive one of the cars and take some sort of command.

Even in the three weeks that she had been with the corps Gipsy had already been dissatisfied with her own position; she felt that so much energy and usefulness was being run to waste for want of proper grip and organization. Nevertheless, she and Mairi knew one thing, for lack of which knowledge so many well-intentioned women fall by the way when they attempt to do hard public work. They knew how to wait. In all work of world importance there are dreary intervals of waiting, and, as Mairi said, "patience is necessary beyond everything." A great many women live on a kind of spurious excitement; they must be rushing from one thing to another, and if this stimulant fails them they collapse altogether. It is the woman who knows how to wait who can take the opportunity when it comes. Therefore, though the first start had not been auspicious, yet Gipsy was willing to wait, for with the additions to the party, and the knowledge born of experience, she was hopeful of better things for the future. It was a new start.

She and Mairi went through their clothes, and discovered that many things that had been considered absolute necessities on leaving were merely encumbrances; so they sent back to England all but

49

the strictest minimum, or what they now considered so. They had passed one milestone on the way, but there were others ahead! Three of the ladies of the party were to work with the forward ambulances in future, collecting the wounded, and the other two, at first, were to remain at the hospital. Naturally there was great competition for the danger-line. Mrs. Knocker, it was unanimously acknowledged, must be a "forward" as, owing to her expert knowledge of cars, she was invaluable. "My driving was much more use than my nursing," she remarked, in speaking of these days; but there were difficulties in placing the rest of the party. It eventually fell to Mairi and the American lady to toss for the last place at the front, and Mairi, to her great joy, won.

Furnes is south of Nieuport, about a third of the way between it and Dunkirk, but further inland than either. It is not a coast town, and is a meeting-place for many canals. Like all these quiet old Belgian towns, it has a Grand Place, and to this day Furnes still embodies something of the restful Sunday-afternoon feeling which was a characteristic of so many of these little towns before they were rudely awakened out of their sleep to be mutilated and smashed. There are two great churches in the Place, and a beautiful Hôtel de Ville with a verandah or balcony in front.

In one corner of the Square are some quaint old Spanish houses with crow-stepped gables and red roofs, in contrast with the grey stone of the other buildings. As the cars rolled in on October 21 the red light of the autumn sun caught these roofs and showed up between the flying buttresses of St. Walburga. The little groups of soldiery standing about gave the impression of terriers with their ears pricked. They wore an air of expectancy; yet Dixmude was held, and while Dixmude remained Furnes was safe.

Year by year on the last Sunday in July the inhabitants of Furnes have turned out in holiday garb to watch, with mingled awe and excitement, the strange procession organized by the *Confrérie de la Sodalité*. Weird men covered by dark brown robes which came over their heads like palls, leaving only two slits for their bright narrowed eyes to peep out, walked solemnly through the streets; they bent beneath burdens of heavy crosses, and their bare feet struck the uneven stones. Yes, and there were women too, thus disguised, doing penance for sins of which their own consciences accused them. They were followed by other oddly dressed characters, which seemed to the startled children, who kept one hand on their mother's gown, to have marched straight out of the Bible.

50

There was Abraham flourishing the very sword with which he prepared to kill Isaac, and Aaron with his snaky rod. Then the hot grip relaxed a little, for there came next a real babe, one that they knew was like themselves. But the awe and the mystery gathered again as they saw Jesus crowned with thorns, stately though in agony, with the sharp points actually pressing into his flesh, and the same Christ bending beneath the cross. Then, as the evening darkened, and the serious mummers, doing their part with intense earnestness and solemnity, paraded round the Square, there appeared the Host, most mysterious of all, with flaming torches and shadowy figures beside it. All these sights were of the nature of a mystery-play, and were reverently carried out by the people themselves: they were not done for purposes of gain or to attract tourists, for very few tourists ever discovered Fumes. With this annual ceremony and the remembrance of the Inquisition in their midst, of which dread stories were whispered, while the very house where those awful torturers sat in conclave is still standing in their sight, the people of Furnes grew up with more of seriousness in their nature than their fellow-subjects.

And now reality had come upon them. What need any more to represent these things in mummery when the *via crucis* was on every highroad in Belgium; when strings of weary men and women, parched with thirst and nearly dead with fear, bowed beneath their loads, trudged solemnly along they knew not whither; when these very churches, so sacred and so grand, St. Walburga with its high steeple and St. Nicholas with its tall, blunt tower, were packed with dying and agonized men suffering from tortures as real as any dealt by the Inquisition? The remembrance of those garbed figures peeping through the slits in their hoods became almost friendly in comparison with the ruddy-faced, brutal German soldier in the hated grey-green uniform. When Furnes revives her Passion-play, it will seem a play indeed against the background of reality.

The convent close up against St. Nicholas is now a hospital, and it was into this courtyard that the cars of the ambulance party turned when they reached their destination. The battle of Dixmude had filled the little rooms with wounded, and even the reading-rooms and the chapel were requisitioned. The courtyard was crowded with the ambulances, and every ten minutes a fresh load of wounded was brought in.

No words can describe the horror of the scene that unrolled before them in the wards. There was so much to be done and so few to do it. The great influx of the wounded had swamped all attempts at order. Those who had just been attended to were lying side by side with the dead, and all the loathsome sights and smells of an operating-theatre were mingled with those of a charnel-house. Some men lay dying silently, the perspiration standing in beads on their foreheads as they gasped for each difficult breath that might be the last; others were hideous spectacles, with smashed faces or lack of limbs. They twisted and groaned in irrepressible agony, uttering low, heart-rending moans that would not be suppressed. Valiantly the whole party of the new-comers set to work to separate the living from the dead, and carry out the bodies to the room set apart for them opposite.

Twice we were called into the operating-room with our stretcher, and twice I received the full weight of a man off the operating-table. I supported the head-end of the stretcher, as I was the stronger, (said Mairi).

The doctors had not a second to lose, or life might be wasted; if a man died, he must be tumbled off hastily to make way for one for whom there might be a chance. The dead were laid out in rows together, some wrapped in winding-sheets; but here and there the uniformity of the still lines was broken by a homely, mud-stained uniform, just as if a soldier had lain down to sleep among them.

For five hours these noble women worked at this terrible task. As fast as the beds in the wards were emptied of their inert burdens they were re-occupied by others, for the ambulances brought in fresh cases continually, and it might be that the next man also died, and was in his turn carried out within the next few moments. Meantime, two small boys with a hand-cart were all the transport available for transferring the bodies from the ever-filling mortuary to the place of burial. The lads took hold of the stretcher, tilted it up a little, slid the dead man into the cart, and when they had as many bodies as they could manage they went off with their load. Thus the men who had stood up for honour and right against an over-whelming foe, who had preferred that their country might for a while be overrun in order that her soul might live forever, were huddled into nameless graves.

There was no room in the already overflowing convent for any of the party to lodge, and so they were told to hunt up quarters for themselves anywhere in the town. Many of the houses were empty, as the inhabitants had fled. A Belgian gentleman who had lost every-thing he possessed by the war had attached himself to the ambulance corps as chauffeur, and when at last Gipsy and Mairi, feeling as if they had been bruised all over, body and soul, with the body-breaking and heart-rending work, were free to think of themselves, they found him waiting.

"You will want somewhere to live; I can show you a house that belonged to my cousin," he said in French. "It has, at all events, a good pianola and is clean."

They followed him gratefully, for to start house-hunting in an unknown town at that hour of the night was a pastime that had no attractions to offer. When they reached the house, he gave them the key and told them to go in and take possession, and himself vanished.

It might have been one of those houses in Pompeii where everyone was eating and drinking and going on with their ordinary avocations when swift death descended on them from the sky. On the table in the dining-room was the horrible *débris* of what had been the last meal, scraps of food lying on the dirty plates where the dust had hardly had time to settle. Flowers still unwilted were in the vases, and the promised pianola was open. As the two tired women penetrated from one room to another they became very silent, and ceased to remark on the familiar evidences of life. It was as if the house were tenanted with ghosts; it was almost impossible to believe that these people who had lived and loved in that place were not there silently resenting the intrusion.

The evacuation must have been in the night, for the beds had obviously been used, and the coverings were hastily flung aside as by those who rise in haste. In the largest bedroom, that of the lady of the house, clothes were lying about on chair-backs and on the floor—dainty delicate garments, in accordance with the dressing-table appointments, and the violet-scented sachet carelessly dropped among them. It was horrible to think of the occupant of that room as a homeless wanderer, possibly dependent on charity!

They could picture the scene. The scepticism as the tale of the oncoming Germans became more insistent; the refusal to go. "They will never come to Furnes," and then the cry ringing through the silence of the night: "Dixmude is fallen; the Germans are almost here." No matter whether the cry were true or false, it pierced like truth into those startled ears, and almost stopped the beating of the heart for an agonized second. Then the thoughts of husband and wife simultaneously leapt to the nursery. "The children!"

This was on the next storey, and the toys of the children proved their presence. They lay on the floor in a pathetic little row. Near the door were a furry bear, a doll without a head, and a cart. It was as if the little ones had snatched up their treasures, and had had them pulled away from them one by one by the frightened nurse. Would they ever return? And what would be their future, torn up by the roots like this? Lucky for them, indeed, if their parents clung tightly to them in that modern Exodus, for if not, it might be that those very children, whose soft little fingers had clung so determinedly to the beloved bear, might be hopelessly lost, as thousands of Belgian children have been, to be brought up in one great group, not knowing their own names or the names of their forbears, forlorn waifs, in spite of all that human kindness could do.

CHAPTER 5

On the Road

There was no question about the amount of work waiting to be done at Furnes. Calls from Dixmude, where hot fighting was going on, were incessant, and the ambulances were kept hard at it. Dixmude is about eight miles south-east of Furnes as the crow flies, but much more by road; and the way along the scattered and smashed *pavé* was rolled out many times in a day by the coming and going of the motors. Chauffeurs were difficult to get, and there were many cars requiring drivers now; so early next morning Gipsy had hardly had time to get on her clothes before there was a shout, and she ran down to find Gilbert waiting outside with the heavy 40 h.p. Napier. There was no one else to take it, and he ordered her to do so. Put upon her mettle, she obeyed at once, but as she climbed into the seat she realized that she did not even know which were the levers for the various gears, for she had never driven that sort of car before. A trifle like that was soon rectified by a few little experiments, and she managed all right. Before she had been in Belgium long she had driven an extraordinary number of different makes of car, including a Daimler, Wolseley, Mercédès, Napier, Pipe, Sunbeam, and Fiat, and she had had to take a great many of them at a moment's notice too.

It was not like driving on an English road, for here the *pavé* in the centre is made of cobbles, and just wide enough for two vehicles to pass each other with care; it slopes down a little at each side, and is usually, in the winter at all events, greasy with a thin layer of mud, whereas, if you fail to hold on, you land in unfathomable depths of mud like thick porridge which borders the sides. Beyond this again there is usually a ditch filled to the brim with water, and with no sort of guard to protect the sides, so that a plunge into icy water is not outside the bounds of possibility. With a top-heavy ambulance the joys of getting off into the mud are enhanced by knowing that it is quite as likely as not that if your wheel goes deep into that quagmire the whole thing may turn right over, a particularly cheerful prospect if it happens to be full of wounded men! At the very best, the feat of regaining the *pavé* entails a tearing strain on a woman's hand and arm. There is a choice of two roads between Furnes and Dixmude. The northern one is more direct, but it was not considered feasible at this time, so the party went by the southern one, turning up by Oudecappelle within sight of Dixmude.

It was the last part of the straight, open road, when they were well within range of the German guns, that strained the nerves most. Mairi was beside her friend on the front of the ambulance, and they were the last of the whole cavalcade, so that if anything had happened to them none of the others would have seen it. Gilbert, who was leading, always went "hell for leather," with a disregard of adverse conditions little less than miraculous, and he never went faster than when he was heading straight for danger. The vile road was broken and pitted with the huge, irregular craters where the shells had fallen. Far ahead was the little bunch of houses, of which some were already burning. Shoved to one side of the route by someone who had had to get off his car to do it was a dead horse on his back, with all his legs in the air in a grotesque parody of a comfortable back-scratching roll. Not far off him was an "awful warning" in the shape of a big car smashed to pieces by a shell which must have landed plump into the middle of it and wiped out of time and space any occupants it contained.

Ahead the firing was like a tropical thunderstorm, with ominous flashes and a deep, menacing growl, and instead of fleeing from it, as would be man's natural instinct, they were steering straight into the heart of it. They could not get actually into Dixmude itself, but reached Caeskerke, where Gilbert, who was in charge of the party, told them to reverse the cars, facing them homewards, ready to plunge off any second. They were up against some small cottages, and about them some of the French soldiers were entrenched, while others lay along the sloping sides of the road along which they had just come. They were there for half an hour watching with a kind of fascination the sharp, stabbing flame, followed by a cloud of white smoke, or a red roar as a shell caught one of the remaining cottages out in the open and sent it up in a furnace of fire.

Nearer and nearer came the warning hiss and scream, until at last they could actually see the pieces flying as the shells burst, exactly as sometimes represented in an illustration, a thing pooh-poohed by those who have never been under shell-fire. Then with a roar and a deafening noise a farm-house not more than fifty yards from them received a shell full upon it, and Gilbert waved a commanding arm ordering them to be gone.

It required more than common nerve to get the engine started in such conditions, but it was achieved at last, and they went back the way they had come, out into the open, passing by a huge new pit that had been made in the last half-hour, a pit which yawned across the way and would easily have swallowed up the whole car.

They drew up near a church about a mile out, and waited here for further orders; they had not been there ten minutes when an armoured car came bumping painfully along with a burst back tyre. Some Belgian officers jumped down, and after standing round for a few minutes in discussion together, one of them advanced, with the fascinating little tassel swinging from his cap as he saluted, and asked if the ladies would take back to Furnes some German prisoners he had in the armoured car, otherwise he did not know what to do with them. It certainly was a strange request to make to a woman not of his own nationality, and the trust implied in her skill and courage was unbounded. Gipsy rose to the occasion at once.

I think it was the proudest moment of my life, (she says in her diary.)

The five Germans, well set up, fair, hard-eyed striplings, were transferred to the ambulance without delay, and as they were installed and the order given to start the two friends saw with a sort of terrified glee that the Belgian officers did not think it necessary to provide an escort; they had too much to do elsewhere. They seemed to take the whole abnormal proceeding very much as a matter of course, and stood in a row and saluted while the two women drove off with the very strangest car-load it had ever been woman's fate to convoy.

Eight miles lay between them and safety, and at any moment, if those unemotional, ruthless young brutes inside had taken it into their heads, they could have got out and knocked the amateur chauffeurs on the head, and escaped with the car. As they went cautiously along this aspect of it was naturally very much to the fore in the minds of the Two on the front seat, and they spoke of it in whispers; but possibly the Germans themselves were glad enough to get safely out of that hell of shot and shell, for they made no attempt at an escape.

The job was accomplished safely, the men handed over to authority, and the car went on to take a load of wounded soldiers to the station. Then, conscious of having accomplished an excellent day's work, the Two returned to their quarters and supped off bully beef and soldier's biscuit. "It was a great day," they said.

In the days that followed they were constantly backwards and forwards on that long and dangerous road, and recognized without difficulty each new shell-hole along the way. The road was so broken in parts that men were sent out with great faggots of wood on their shoulders to throw into the holes and fill them up, and constant repairing was necessary to keep the route open for the heavy military transport. All this work in the open air, with hard physical lifting and driving, took it out of the Two so much that they were always thankful, when the day's work was done, to get back and drop into bed—a real bed, too, a great luxury in those times.

A few other members of the party were installed in the same house, but Mairi and Gipsy retained their bedroom to themselves. They were usually able to obtain food at the hospital, where they fared very simply. Porridge for breakfast was acceptable, and occasionally fried potatoes were added, if they had time to cook them and they did not get spoiled just as they were ready, which is the way of potatoes in the hands of amateur cooks all the world over. "These" porridge must have felt gratified at its appreciation; even in Scotland, where it is ennobled by the use of the plural number, it can rarely have been referred to as "a joyful basin of porridge!"

The night work was perhaps the greatest strain, for there could of course be no lights, and the way was lit up grimly by the sudden flare of the exploding shells, or the dim light of distant buildings which they had set on fire. It was a curious sight to see the roof of one of these huge torches collapse suddenly, apparently in absolute silence, for the ceaseless cannonade drowned all lesser sounds; then the flames would shoot up like a great cascade of fireworks, brightening everything for hundreds of yards around, and illuminating the great holes cut in the road till they appeared like an irregular procession of monstrous tortoises who had eaten the "Food of the Gods."

Sometimes so many of these devil's fires were alight at once that they brought back a reminiscence of bonfires on Coronation night. "Farmhouses burning, trees burning, everything burning. It was a grand sight, and one I shall never forget," says Mairi enthusiastically. And in the midst of that great amphitheatre set for a life and death drama Luck and Fate stalking alongside, determined that these particular actors should live to play a great part.

The effect of the shells, even on the presumably tough chauffeurs, was eloquent of the nerve-racking strain. One man was perfectly ill with it, and yet he had the right sort of pluck, for he owned up to the cause of his malady, but set his teeth and went on in grim determination. He stuck to his wheel one day, when he was driving Mrs. Knocker, until he became fairly paralyzed, and was manifestly unable to go on, so she changed places with him and took the driving-wheel herself. They were carrying four wounded men, and she brought them into safety, and then said she must go back, as she had left Mairi at Oudecappelle, but that as he was feeling ill he had better stay at Furnes. He looked at her with a face that was like the face of one of the dead in the convent wards, and said doggedly through stiff lips:

Can't drive, but I ain't going to give in to it. I'm coming back right alongside of you this very minute.

She could not but admire this heroic triumph of mind over matter.

Poor fellow! When we turned the corner of the road and got within range of those big guns, and each flash could be clearly seen, he turned suddenly sick, and I had to stop and give him brandy and cover him with a rug. I begged him not to look. It is a sight which requires a peculiar kind of nerves.

She does not add that it requires a kind of courage so peculiar that it is rare indeed!

It was getting dusk, and those great bulbs of flame were horribly vivid, and everywhere the masses of farm-buildings or haystacks showed their effect. The continuous deafening noise was killing, and always above the deep bass of the guns the high alto of the screaming shells never ceased for one instant. It seemed as if it were too frightful to continue for another second, yet if it stopped suddenly one's skull would fall to pieces!

It was no wonder that some of the chauffeurs, who were mostly very young and raw, could hardly face it. They did not do badly considering. It was the custom for the heavy ambulances to be left outside the worst firing, in what might be called the penumbra of the danger-zone, and then the light scout cars were run up into the hotter places to retrieve the wounded. No one was forced to go on this service;

volunteers were called for, and among these volunteers were always the women of the party. Just at first of course, they, like the men, were quite ignorant of the fearful danger, and went forward with the excited interest of children into the battlefield; but soon, very soon, their eyes were opened, and they knew what it meant. It was then, when the danger was fully recognized, that the pull came!

One young Cockney chauffeur, called Tom, was among the bravest of the brave, and did more than his share, because, besides going fearlessly and light-heartedly into the very mouth of the inferno, he exercised a dry turn of humour, which helped the others through better, possibly, than anything else could have done. It often just tipped the balance the right way when it was swinging dangerously. After all, risky as the fire-zone was, it was quite a question among them whether it was not more risky in another way to stay in the ill-ventilated, overcrowded hospital, with its primitive lack of sanitary arrangements.

The Furnes folk were still in that happy state of simplicity when anything out of sight is considered harmless. It was Tom who expressed the British view when, on coming suddenly one day into the poisonous atmosphere after the freshness of a rush through the air, he exclaimed: "My, but them drines is just crude! Give me busting shells all the time-o."

On the evening in question Mairi had been sitting on a wall in Oudecappelle, waiting for the return of the car, with a few soldiers and one or two peasants to keep her company. She, as well as Gipsy, always had a feeling that it was less dangerous to be out of doors under shell-fire, or, at any rate, that it was preferable to meet death, if it must be met, under the full sail of the sky, rather than the flat straitness of roof and walls. So Mairi sat there in charge of some wounded men who lay just inside the door of a cottage, and she watched the shells getting heavier and heavier. The French and Belgian batteries were quite near, and were answering the challenge of the foe madly, and altogether there was no lack of liveliness.

Then some of the soldiers, hurrying up, told her that the Germans were coming—the same old cry—and that they themselves had been ordered further down the road; but the girl only smiled sweetly, and went to look at her charges to be sure that everything was ready for immediate transportation when the ambulance should arrive. And as she went out again to look for its coming another ambulance drove up from the opposite direction, and from it stepped out a man of medium height, with a keen, laughing face and those glinting eyes that carry a signal of personal fearlessness even to the least observant. No wonder he looked a little surprised to find this fair-haired girl, so very young and not over big, in charge by herself in the gathering dusk, at this place, which in a danger competition would have gained high marks. He had just come from Dixmude himself, which would certainly in such a competition have been more successful still.

So he began to talk to Mairi with a warm degree of comradeship, and just then Gipsy drove up, with the exhausted chauffeur beside her, as miserable and ashamed as a man could be. Dr. Van der Ghinst thereupon introduced himself, bowing gracefully, and held out to the Two a rose apiece, telling them laughingly that they were the last roses in Dixmude, where he was working at the hospital of St. Jean, looking after the wounded. As Dixmude was then about the centre of the vortex, and most of the houses were either fallen or tottering, he did not lack exhilaration in his daily routine. Brave spirits all the world over have something in common, and these three fraternized at once. There was no need of introductions; they knew each other, for their hearts were set on the same thing.

The doctor was evacuating his wounded, who had to be taken over all the long road to Furnes, with the result that many died by the way, and, looking at them pitifully, an idea which had been germinating for some time in Gipsy's brain suddenly took form. Why should there not be a dressing-station close up to the lines at the front? Could not many lives be saved if the wounded could have immediate rest and care, so as to neutralize the effects of shock and fortify them for what they had to go through in the way of weary journeying and knocking about? At present, many a man died from a comparatively slight wound, because his system was utterly exhausted by shock and he had no strength left. While they were still discussing the project, from which extraordinary results were to spring, a French marine came in screaming with pain; two of his fingers had been severed, and he sobbed and groaned so heart-rendingly that, though they were getting a little hardened, it almost unstrung Mrs. Knocker.

It was still raining hard when, tired out, the two friends returned to their house. It was quite lonely, no other member of the party being there at the time. They found the back-door open and the glass panels smashed. As they stood for a second looking at one another in surprise, they could hear the distant rumble of the guns and the immediate drip and splutter of the rain running down in spouts from the roof. They slowly penetrated into the empty house, not knowing what they might not meet. The front-door also stood wide open, and it looked as if whoever had been there had hastily escaped that way on hearing their approach. However, they searched everywhere, and, having found no sign of anyone, at last literally dropped asleep as they undressed, tumbling into bed dead-beat.

The next morning they were still in bed when they heard a knock at the door, and when Mairi, huddling on a coat, opened it she was confronted by a burly French soldier, who looked uncommonly sheepish. He explained hurriedly and with his eyes anywhere but on her face that he wanted his revolver. "But I have not got your re-volver," said Mairi, too surprised for words. "Gipsy, here's a man who wants his revolver—at least, I think that's what he wants, unless there is some other French word which sounds exactly like it."

But it was his *revolver* he inquired for steadily, and when they pressed him to say where it was, and why he thought they had got it, his eyes roved more wildly than before as he blurted out, "*C'est dans votre lit, mesdemoiselles*"

Hastily they turned back to the bed, but the man slipped past them, and, putting his grimy hand beneath the pillow, drew forth his heavy revolver. Gipsy snatched it from him. "You shan't have it until you tell us how it came there," she cried, in mingled amusement and indigna-tion; so he confessed that he and the other soldiers who were about the place, and had no regular quarters, used to come and sleep here in the daytime, because they knew the ladies were always out till late. "*Ça ne fait rien, et c'est bien confortable*," he ended, gripping the revolver and grinning as he rushed out.

French soldiers sleeping in the bed by daytime! Only those who have been among soldiers will understand what that means. It ex-plained so many things!

CHAPTER 6

Gipsy and the Major

By this time the resources of food at the hospital had run out—even porridge was not available—but fortunately one small butcher's shop in the town was discovered open, and at the back was a kind of little cafe where the workers could get something to eat. Through the streets of Furnes they went night by night in the pitch darkness, occasionally brightened by an odd gleam that seemed to come from nowhere until you were right on the top of it and looked down into a cellar opening off the pavement, where some of the few inhabitants who had not fled were crouching together talking in awestruck tones by the gleam of a candle or a few sticks. All lights were strictly suppressed of course, and at first, when there was still a certain amount of meat in the butcher's shop, they had to grope their way out, knocking their faces against the cold, still carcasses that hung suspended stiffly from their hooks.

As for the provender they got, Mairi remarks caustically of the soup: "One tomato in fifteen pints of water, but it was hot."

In desperation she and Gipsy at last descended to the cellars of the house they were in, and found some potatoes, jam, beer, and bottled waters, and carried them back for all to share alike. They had certainly earned their keep by the work they were doing for the Belgians.

Dixmude was being steadily shelled, and day by day they went on that long, dangerous road to bring in all the survivors they could. But the day's work was not unrelieved tragedy; a note of high comedy was struck the day Gipsy happened to be out in Oostkerke, about four miles west of Dixmude, just off the more direct and northerly road between that place and Furnes. She had made friends with a very odd-looking Belgian Major who, if he had been a little larger, would have done, without any making-up, for the figure of the giant in the old nursery tales, for he had a rubicund face, brilliant red hair, and a flaming moustache and bristly eyebrows of the same hue—therefore the word that fitly describes him is "scarlet." He was on observation duty. The only possible places in this flat country from which any extent of ground can be surveyed are the tall steeples of the churches, or, rather, perhaps they *were* the only places, for as both sides made the same discovery, and used them for the identical purpose whenever they came across them, they were naturally shelled persistently, and few indeed survive. The stout major knew no English, but he was greatly impressed by this good-looking, fearless Englishwoman in her war-stained khaki suit, and so, with expressive gestures, he invited her to climb up the church steeple and see for herself where it was that he spent his days surveying. Gipsy never refused an offer like that, especially when the church tower might any moment be crumpled up by a shell. As Miss May Sinclair has said, "she had an irresistible inclination toward the greatest possible danger."

Up they climbed, and as they mounted each ladder became steeper and narrower than the last. When they gained the summit and peered out of the tiny observation hole, shells were bursting around in a way to satisfy the most ardent lover of danger! As they descended, in a very steep and narrow place, the major stopped, completely barring the way, and drawing from his pocket a little crumpled French-English dictionary, laboriously turned the pages with his thick moistened thumb until he had found what he wanted. Then, looking up, he spluttered out: "*Si je n'étais pas marié. Je voudrais dire,* 'I luv you.'"

A sense of her own appalling loss must have made Gipsy nearly fall from her perch; it certainly required every bit of her self-control to enable her to keep her countenance and insist on his proceeding. But she had plenty of dignity, and the descent, perilous in more ways than one, was safely accomplished. They descended again, to find at the church door a sight which straightway sent the matter flying from her head. A French officer lay there with his foot in "a lovely mess." He had been scouting along the railway line which runs through Oostkerke, between Furnes and Dixmude, and a bullet had gone clean through his leg low down. He dropped on the ground to apply his first-aid bandage, and suddenly a "Black Maria" burst within ten yards of him, throwing earth all over his bleeding wound. He knew the great danger of the microbes in the soil getting into an open wound, and, having nothing else handy, he used the contents of his flask, which happened to be coffee, to wash it out. But as he told the story he was concerned,

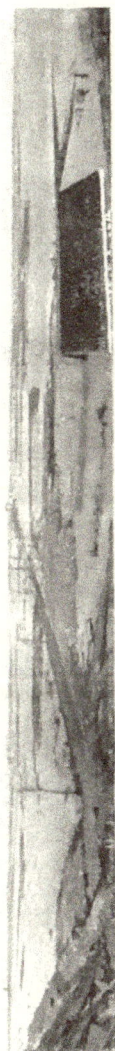

What they looked at for many months

The Pervyse graveyard.

A ruined house in Pervyse

not with the pain of the wound, or with the terribly narrow escape he had had of his life, but with indignation that the shell should have dared to spatter him and make him waste his precious coffee! Such is human nature! He had dragged himself back to shelter with his mind full of this detestable outrage, and he poured it forth to a most sympathetic listener. Gipsy attended to him skilfully, and helped him into the little dugout occupied by the major. But directly she had entered it she was filled with anxiety to get out in a hurry; such a smell of stale tobacco, burnt fat, and other worse odours, permeated the place that it might be imagined even a shell would rebound harmlessly off the solidity of the atmosphere! However, nothing would satisfy the major but that she must sit down and have a plate of soup. In whatever circumstances, soup did sound inviting on this bitter day to someone chronically underfed and overtired, so she assented.

A plate was promptly produced containing soup of a pale yellow colour, with a layer of grease about half an inch thick on the top. It was accompanied by a spoon which had most obviously been used to "sup soup" by someone else a very short time before. However, Gipsy philosophically remarks, "It looked a little cleaner when it had been in my soup!"

While she was struggling with the mess heroically, unwilling to hurt the feelings of her well-meaning host, his face lit as a happy thought struck him, and, fumbling in his pocket, he produced a little silver-paper pill, which he crushed between his fingers, burying it gaily and firmly in the midst of the plate of soup. The awful thought that it might be some sort of love-potion—nothing seemed too weird for belief in the strange life she now led—seized on Gipsy, and her quick mind visioned a sort of *Midsummer Night's Dream*, with the major in the part of Bottom! Seeing that he was delighted with his own performance, and totally unaware of the feelings he was arousing in her, even while she watched the soup grow darker under the influence of the pill, she nobly swallowed more of the nauseous compound. The taste assured her that the addition must have been some sort of *Liebig*, and the worst consequences would not result!

In came just then a doctor belonging to the corps, and he was straightway supplied with a similar plate; and as he looked at it wonderingly, and Gipsy thrust hers from her, having had all that human nature could endure, the little major thereupon crowned his achievements by snatching at the spoon and picking up by its aid what was left of the silver pill—mainly paper by this time—and conveying it and the spoon together into the soup of the newcomer!

The second course of this appetizing meal was a stale and decrepit-looking piece of steak that had evidently won through with its life after a fierce assault by someone. This was too much; good intention carries far, but beyond a point flesh revolts. Gipsy shook her head as pleasantly as she could, but with a decision that was unmistakable, where-upon, the little man, dancing round her in the confined space, hauled out his precious dictionary, and after a mad hunt found the elusive words he was searching for, and with flaming face and eyes thrust them under her nose:

"I am stung to the quick!"

CHAPTER 7

A Hideous Night Drive

Dixmude was in a terrible state, suffering from a blasting and withering shell-fire, yet there the ambulances went on, hearing that wounded men needed them. They did not stop short of the town itself this time, but went right in. "We worked there all day and all night."

The streets were heaps of *débris*. Whole walls had fallen flat; others were cracked by great diagonal fissures, and were ready to fall at any moment and bury the party, who crashed along anyhow over huge upturned paving-stones and masses of brick rubble. Every now and again a shell landed somewhere, hitting a house fair and square, and reducing it to the same condition as hundreds of others, which had already lost all semblance of houses; when this occurred a Gargantuan puff of black smoke rose, and on its evaporation, behold, the house was no more!

At one place the whole of such a house had slid down across the street, and when the first car arrived at the obstacle the chauffeur looked at the leader for instructions. "Go over it," he said, and the man, with wonderful pluck, did so, landing with a tremendous jolt and crash on the other side. At first the place seemed deserted, but as they advanced hasty figures diving round corners and disappearing in by-streets showed more and more frequently, and at last the first impression was completely wiped out—the place seemed alive with Belgian and French soldiers. The wounded had been collected at the splendid Town Hall, the building which means so much more to Continental nations than it does to us. The mighty pillars at the entrance had fallen this way and that, and one standing grandly upright recalled the majesty of a ruined Egyptian temple.

It was not the wounded only that were to be saved; there were still some few miserable inhabitants living in the haunted desolation, and by peeping down into gaping cellars, and calling softly to see if any living thing would respond, at last four or five old women of ages between eighty and ninety were discovered huddled together, waiting for death. One of these poor old things had had her hand badly hurt; it had been roughly bandaged some four days before, and had remained uncleansed and unchanged since, so that the wound was in a horrible state. But she did not seem to mind the pain; only as Gipsy attended to her gently she started jabbering hard and very fiercely, as if she was angry about something. As it was a stream of Flemish, nothing was intelligible. Gipsy called to a Flemish soldier outside to come in and interpret, and when he had asked a few questions of the excited old crone he laughed carelessly, and explained in French: "It's all right, Sister; she is only upset because a wisp of her hair is hanging down and she can't get her hands up to tidy it, and she doesn't think she's fit for you to see." So the long wisp of lanky grey hair had to be tenderly fastened back before the dressing proceeded.

The dash into Dixmude was followed by a terrible discovery—M. de Broqueville, who had been in charge, was missing. He had given the order to start back, and then, when the cars had got clear of the town, it was found that he was not with them. After the wounded had been safely landed attempts were unsuccessfully made to find him, but it was not until the next day he turned up smiling, walking quietly in among his comrades, mercifully unhurt. It appeared he had made a dash down a cellar to help someone at the last minute, and when he came up found the cars had gone. He had actually walked back along the shell-torn road and escaped without a scratch.

It was nearly the end of October when the first warnings came that Furnes in its turn might have to be evacuated. The great grey host, like a swarm of locusts, was advancing on the unhappy country; thousands had been killed, but there seemed always to be thousands more to take their places. The gallant defenders had nobly played their part, and it must be remembered that they were really more like a trained civil force than an army, for Belgium had had no reason to expect war. They had performed prodigies of valour, nobly backed up by the plucky little French marines and Senegalese. Further to the south, at Ypres, the British had come to the rescue, but the Belgians themselves must have the credit for holding the most western extremity of the line, helped by the British naval guns as the enemy came within range. Some of their feats are worthy of the best traditions of a military nation. They had dashed with armoured cars right into the heart of the enemy's host, spurting leaden death, and retiring unharmed themselves; some of these tales read like the stories of knights in armour attacking dragons in the old days.

But the huge soulless machine in opposition was only scratched by such episodes, not injured. The immensity of it was past all calculation. Its efficiency was the result of years of concentration, and the discipline of the units was such that they were merged in one welded mass; no man had a soul of his own. Stories of the irresistible momentum of this compact mass, of its appliances for continuing and enduring and filling up gaps, its horrible persistency when beaten back again and again, had swelled and gathered, and terror grew. Small wonder was it then, when a few shells fell in Furnes, that imagination quickened its approach. The few people who had not already gone began to go post-haste. It had come within the range of possibility that the hideous cruelties and loath-some brutalities enacted at Louvain and Dinant, Aerschot and other towns, might even be the fate of Furnes. All night long the streets rumbled with departing vehicles, mingled with the clatter of advancing cavalry hoofs, and as a background the roll of the guns gathered force and sounded ominously nearer. Even the ambulance people were warned to leave, but they determined to "stick it out" so long as they could be useful.

On the morning of October 29, Gipsy and Mairi got up as usual at six. They washed in that "half-teaspoonful" of water to which they had grown accustomed. Water was very scarce in Furnes, and Gipsy remarks casually, "I am so dirty, I feel I shall soon walk without legs!"

The British field hospital had taken a different view of the situation from the members of the ambulance corps, and had gone south at the sound of the alarm. The leaders had already once experienced what it meant to wait to the last minute, and knew what it had cost them, and so were determined not to be caught again. There was an atmosphere of horrible uncertainty everywhere, the confusion of a war seen from the middle instead of from the end.

Yet the cars ran out to Oudecappelle as usual among the dead bodies of horses and cows that lined that road. Some of these had been cut up, and the joints taken for food; others had reached the stage of being pestilential. Gipsy was driving, and rifle-bullets, always a sign of an advance, had begun to hum. She sheltered beside the wall of a house, which does form some protection from this form of attack, though none from shell-fire, and she amused herself by remarking the different notes of the bullets. When one struck anything it made a little smack like the crack of a well-manipulated whip, because the displaced air cracks at the sharp end of the flight.

Most of the day was given over to a vague running about hither and thither without much result, and the atmosphere was full of a maddening suspense. At last a message came for someone to go out to an outlying post to fetch in wounded men. This could only be done under cover of darkness. So as soon as the dusk came down in a kindly veil several of the party started. Tom was driving the first car, and had Mairi with him, among others; whilst Gipsy drove the second, the big Napier ambulance. This still retained its glass screen, and as it was raining the screen became blurred and added to the difficulty of seeing ahead. It was a matter of crawling along foot by foot in the grease of the *pavé*. Thus they went to Caeskerke, close to Dixmude, where the Germans might break through at any moment according to reports.

When they came to the cross-roads Gipsy received orders to turn to the left, while the first car went to the right. The first party picked up a number of Senegalese very quickly and took them back to Furnes. Gipsy crawled over the ground at a walking pace toward a lonely farm, where she had been told she would find cases to bring back. The surface was so greasy that the wheels would hardly hold the road at all, but there was a fair light from a village in flames some way off. The farmhouse had been used as a depot for the wounded, and they were being brought in thick and fast. When she arrived here the whole available space in the ambulance was quickly filled with stretcher cases. Mr. G——, an American who had done good work with the ambulance, climbed inside the car to help the men whose hold on life was slipping from them, and all alone on that front seat sat one frail woman to guide to safety that huge, heavy car which resembled a motor-bus.

The roads were abominable; never had she known them so bad. Sometimes the steering-wheel was jerked right out of her hands, which, for all their skill, had not the strength to hold up the weight so suddenly thrown upon the wrists. The skids were almost continuous, and jerked the living freight from side to side. At any moment the whole ambulance might topple right over. She had been driving off and on since seven that morning, and was already tired. Her back ached to agony, her eyeballs were strained with trying to pierce the grisly darkness.

The blaze of the burning village died down until only a red glow remained. All at once a shell burst as it seemed right overhead, and in the blinding light she saw something straight across the track, something big and black, which made her shut down the brakes and pull up. Then she could see nothing with that flashing light still repeating itself in her eyes and making the red dusk seem velvet-black; so, after waiting a minute, she clambered down from the seat and felt about with her hands, and ascertained that the body of a great cart-horse was lying across the way. It was far beyond her strength to move, so, groping in the mud, she measured the space left in which to pass, and found she could do it with six inches to spare, but the miscalculation of the six inches would land them all in an awful catastrophe!

However, there was nothing else for it: these precious lives inside depended on her; so, bitterly cold and soaked to the skin, she crept back to the steering-wheel and essayed the difficult task. Inch by inch she crept past, judging the distance, and as her pupils widened she was enabled to see a little, and then she breathed once more as she gained the *pavé*, which, compared with the mud at the side, seemed safety. But she was not by any means out of the wood, for not a quarter of a mile further her groping sight revealed another black mass, this time so big that it was visible without the aid of a shell-burst. Once more she had to get down and investigate; it proved to be a shell-hole quite large enough to swallow the whole ambulance and its contents. Once more she had to carry out unaided that manoeuvring process with so little margin of safety.

When back again on the road she almost ran into a compact group of cavalry that was coming with uncanny silence toward Dixmude. The back-ground of constant noise obliterated all lesser sounds. She warned the men of the shell-hole and passed on. But the end was not yet. According to agreement, she was to return to Furnes by way of Oudecappelle, where Gilbert was waiting. Numbed and trembling with the shocking strain, she felt a momentary relief when she alighted beside his dark figure. Her muscles were wrenched and her hands were shaking, but here was Gilbert without a car, and possibly he would take over the driver's job. She waited silently.

"How many have you got ?" he asked in French.

"It is full inside; there is no room—except"—as an afterthought— "two sitting cases could come alongside me on the front."

"Then you must go back at once and fetch two sitting cases. There are two waiting, slightly wounded, along that road you came. I will show you where."

"I felt as if my heart would burst," Gipsy says, when recounting this incident in her diary.

But what could she do? She was under orders, and her high spirit would have forced her on like a mettled horse until she dropped dead.

With a little choke, but without a word of protest, she turned the car and proceeded to re-traverse that awful road, with Gilbert sitting on the step beside her as a guide. They found the wounded men and placed them in front, and then returned. The road was being shelled heavily now, doubtless because the Germans anticipated reinforcements coming along it. The whistling scream of the great shells, like the scream of a railway engine as it dashes through a station, got nearer and nearer, and even Gilbert himself ducked involuntarily as one burst within ten yards of them, whereat the patient driver smiled a little in the dark. She was far past minding shells herself, voluntarily or involuntarily.

"To get the car along at all, I had to brace every muscle to breaking-point, and every nerve in my body was strung taut. My head ached from straining my eyes in that drizzle, my arms ached from clutching that heavy wheel. There were moments when I felt I *could* not go on, and yet I knew I *must*, and so I did."

On reaching Oudecappelle again, Gilbert alighted and rejoined his own car, which had come back, and for the fifteen miles or so homeward the whole burden of responsibility again fell on this indomitable woman.

How the miles were passed over she did not know. She almost reached the point of insensibility, working like an automaton without feeling before the end; but she came to life on reaching Furnes, and the coming alive was agony. At the entrance into the courtyard of the convent there is almost a right-angled turn up through the gates, a tricky task at the best of times. When she reached it her weak, strained wrist refused to do it. The car had to be stopped, backed, and the chauffeur tried again, failed; tried once more, yet more feebly, and failed again; and then, utterly done, she fell forward on the steering-wheel and for the first time in her life broke down. Faithful little Mairi, who had come home with Gilbert's car and not gone out again, was waiting and watching, and sprang to help her and take her indoors while others brought in the car. No wonder Gipsy says in her diary, "It was one of the most appalling experiences of my life!"

In going through these days of horror during the crisis at Dixmude one is struck with the miraculous way in which the party were preserved. Never shirking, hardly ever out of danger, yet not one of them was hit; they were certainly watched over by a Higher Power.

One time, when they were at Oudecappelle awaiting cases to take home, it seemed quite an ordinary thing to M. de Broqueville to suggest to Gipsy that they should walk up the shell-strewn road after having left the ambulances—just as natural as if he had asked her to go for a stroll in a country lane to wile away the time until the horse had had a feed at a country inn. And it seemed quite as natural to her to accept. She made no comment on the astounding proposition. She simply went.

They could see the shapeless observation balloons of the Germans floating ahead, and Gipsy airily chaffed her companion about the gold tassel on his cap, saying that as it bobbed up and down in the rare gleam of sunlight they were enjoying it made a beacon for the hostile fire. She had hardly said it, and they were about a hundred yards along the road, when a German shell burst in a field on the left; so their pleasant little stroll had to be abruptly curtailed, and they turned to go back. Then a shell sailed straight toward them. They heard it coming, and knew well from experience that the sound portended a very near thing. They stopped dead, waiting tensely through that second that might be the last scrap of time left to them, and the shell pitched not fifteen yards away, covering them both with a pall of dust.

"*Ne bougez pas,*" M. de Broqueville counselled, in his wise, kind, unalarmed tones. So Gipsy stood waiting quietly. Just ahead of them was an old, old peasant man whom they had passed pushing along a barrow full of turnips, and as the "*Ne bougez pas*" rang out he, too, stopped where he was and raised his withered hand to wipe his forehead. The third shell flew screeching overhead, and burst in the ditch by the side of the road, sending up a great spout of water like a geyser. The splinters flew far and wide. One pierced Gipsy's coat, but left her uninjured; and when the smoke died away they saw that the old peasant had fallen forward across his barrow. They sprang forward to help him, and found a splinter had caught him in the back, and it was all over with him.

Having once started, the two ran back toward the cottages where the ambulances were, and as they ran two more shells broke close to them, one smashing an empty cottage into a heap. It had occurred to them both that with the deadly missiles bursting around like this the precious ambulances must be in danger, and must be secured at any cost; so they backed them off three hundred yards along the road, and returned with stretchers to pick up the wounded, for one of the doctors was injured, and a sergeant had had an arm blown off.

After this episode Gipsy remarks severely: "Shells are not things one likes at all. Anyone who *says* he likes them is certainly not speaking the truth."

CHAPTER 8

The Great Idea

The brilliant idea which Gipsy had conceived the day she met Dr. Van der Ghinst grew like Jack's beanstalk, one night at Oudecappelle, when for the first time the two friends together slept among the soldiers in the fire-zone. They had been up and down, up and down, under the direction of Gilbert, almost all day, and when they heard their services would possibly be required at night too, it seemed the obvious thing to do to sleep at this tiny village instead of going back that long, weary way to Furnes. The French marines were occupying a wee *café*, and as one of them advanced to ask the ladies to share it with them, they thought for the moment he was suffering from some new and horrible kind of wound, because he never looked the same for two seconds together; as a matter of fact, he had a face of the *gutta-percha* variety, and in his civilian days had earned many a penny by displaying this eccentricity, of which he was obviously proud. He did not want to let his talent rust for want of use, and so as he came forward he displayed one moment a large, flat, vacant-looking visage, with two tiny eyes like currants, and the next it was shrunk and wizened up as if he had lived to the end of all time.

They watched, fascinated, until he turned and led the way to shelter. This was a very low, dirty little Flemish house with a filthy stained wooden table, greasy soiled chairs, and a floor which might have belonged to a cow-byre. Two chairs were pulled out and put in a corner, and here the two friends sat together, while, as dusk gathered, the gloom was lightened by a guttering candle stuck in a wine-bottle. Just behind them was a Belgian battery, and the heavy guns sent out a roar every few seconds which shook the tumble-down place, so that it was marvellous it did not fall in a heap. Every scrap of glass in the small window-panes had long since vanished. The French soldiers were sitting in the filthy damp straw on the ground, smoking and chatting, spitting, and playing cards with a pack on which the stains looked like a weird new variety of suits.

The place was fairly stuffy, but every now and then the door opened to let in an icy draught. "Rubber Face," as they had christened him, noticed that his guests had nothing with them in the way of food, and in his large-hearted generosity immediately did his best to provide for them. He produced an egg from his pocket with the air of doing a conjuring trick—as indeed it was, for Heaven alone knew how he had managed to keep that egg unbroken since he had obtained it. One would have thought the concussion of the guns would have been enough to shatter it. He promised an omelette, and finding an old tin plate, which he assured them had "*déjà de la graisse*," he broke the egg on to it, holding it over an improvised fire. He would have probably died of a broken heart if they had refused it, and being out to heal and not to break, they had to go through with it.

They wondered what would happen when sleeping-time came. It would be a weary performance to sit upright all night, and yet to fall upon that wet and fetid straw, among the French soldiers, many of whom were heartily asleep already, seemed equally impossible. But Gilbert, by exploring, discovered a small inner room and managed to procure a certain amount of fairly clean straw, and there they retired. It was indeed to Mairi not the first experience of such a kind, because a night or two before, when Gipsy had gone over to Dunkirk, she had slept here alone among the men with the fearless freedom of a child. She had had her own pile of straw in the corner, and was hedged in by Gilbert and Tom, the trustworthy chauffeur. They had had some cushions from the car as pillows, and a couple of rugs, and she says, "I was well protected, for Gilbert had his revolver under his pillow, and lay between me and the soldiers."

It speaks highly indeed for the men that her confidence was justified. And in all the most difficult circumstances arising out of the crude conditions these two women encountered, there is never once a hint that they were annoyed in any way. Mairi had lain down now with her knitted khaki wool cap pulled well down to prevent the straw from tickling her ears, and she was asleep within five minutes. Like the soldiers, she had become so much accustomed to the thunder of the guns that she hardly heard it. But Gipsy was more highly strung, and she found sleep impossible. There was a faint gleam from the candle, which burnt all night, and though she tried hard to sleep, at first

77

she found it out of the question; her imagination was too active.

> The place was so eerie and small, and the rats worried me. I thought of all sorts of stories of rats eating one's nose and nibbling one's finger-nails. The men through the doorway snored, too, horribly. I wondered what would happen if the Germans came suddenly, as they might quite easily do. The springing to life of those slumbering men, and the awful carnage there would be in that tiny space!

It was only when there was a lull in the firing for a moment that the snores could be heard; they were ordinarily drowned in the hullabaloo. When there was a louder crash than usual, so that Gipsy started up thinking the whole house was coming down to bury them, not one of the sleepers stirred. So she sat up and wrote her diary, the little green book that accompanied her everywhere, and was stained and soiled with the weather, matching the red one that Mairi faithfully carried and looked upon as an inestimable confidant. To have the privilege of seeing those two diaries is to get a peep into two uncommonly fine souls, of very different and in many ways complementary characteristics.

At 2.30 Gipsy got up to creep outside to see if anything was happening, and as she moved her girl companion stirred, turned, and flung back the cap from her fair hair and opened her sleepy eyes; so they crept out together. There they stood, feeling very, very small under the arch of that immense plain, with the flashes on the horizon, the red glare over devastated Dixmude, and a bitter wind sweeping around. It was impossible not to recall the solemn words of the prophet Isaiah: "*Your country is desolate, your cities are burned with fire: your land, strangers devour it in your presence.*"

The solemnity of the night, with Death stalking close at hand ready to spring upon them at any second, impressed them. What was going to happen in the future? Were they prepared to go on with this work in spite of all the dirt and rats and smells? Were they able to say to each other fearlessly and confidently;

> I will go through with it; I will devote myself to helping the little soldier in the trenches, whatever comes. No more will I think of myself. I will sleep whenever and wherever I can. I will live, if need be, under fire as he lives. I will carry my life lightly if I can succour, help, and comfort him?

The glamour had all evaporated; they knew what such a vow involved, but quite steadily they both agreed to take it. There were no heroics; there was no romance; there, in that bitter wind, standing in front of the poor little house full of snoring soldiers, with that horrible glare in their eyes, and the thunder of the guns shaking the ground they stood on, they held each other's hands, and determined to thrust away all idea of fears, nerves, or feminine weaknesses. In the early grey light of the morning they consummated that heroic resolve with a real sacrifice. They saw it must be; there was no escaping it. So, with a pair of surgical scissors, Mairi cut and hacked and chopped until she had shorn her friend's dark silky hair to a length of about two inches all round, and then Gipsy did the same for the strong fair crop so unlike her own. They looked at it, laughing queerly, the fair and the dark, before they knotted the tresses together and sent them floating down the canal. When one is grown up, hair completely cut off can never grow quite the same again. Later on, recounting how little one member of the party had really done for the cause, Mairi remarks significantly, "*She* never cut off her hair."

They pulled down their woolly caps well over their shorn heads, so that the men should not notice anything, and returned to the hut. Gipsy says, "With that little bundle of hair went all our nervousness, all our fear of rats, our dislike of dirty food, and our ideas of home comforts. We became soldiers from that hour."

It was very shortly after this that they met Dr. Van der Ghinst again. He had stuck to his wounded in Dixmude until the Germans actually came into the town and took him prisoner; but he was allowed to continue his work, which he did for three days, and then, when he went out to the German trenches under escort to collect the wounded, he managed to give his captors the slip, and, after it was dark, got clear away.

During the many hours of waiting since they had first met him, Mrs. Knocker had thought out many things. It seemed to her that a great deal of the ambulance work was running to waste; there was too much careering backwards and forwards, with too little result. Huge ambulances, consuming a great deal of petrol, were sent on trivial errands. One night she and Mairi had been ordered miles away with a great car merely to carry a bundle of bandages. At another time she had actually been asked to take out "sightseers" from England in one of the cars.

It was after the wounded were collected that the shaking up over

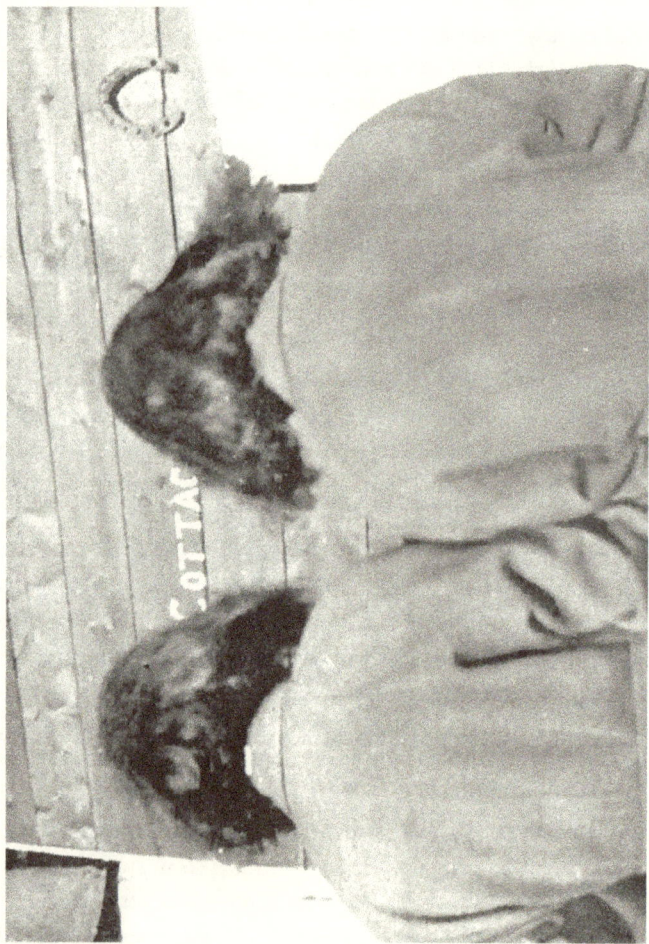

"THE TWO" AFTER HAVING SACRIFICED THEIR HAIR

the vile roads, and the long interval before they could be properly attended to, often resulted in death. There must surely be some way of preventing this. It seemed to Gipsy that a *poste de secours* right up as near to the firing-line as possible, where the men could be treated for shock, and restored somewhat before they had to undergo the awful journey, would be the means of saving many. The question was whether such a *poste* was feasible. Dr. Van der Ghinst warmly approved the idea, but he stood alone, for when it was mooted to the rest of the Corps it met with disapproval all round. Dr. Munro, indeed, told Mrs. Knocker plainly that if she did this she would do it in disobedience to his orders, and all funds would cease—she must finance herself. Ambulance work had the *cachet* of respectability; everyone knew what it was, and approved of it; but this other—whoever in their senses had heard of women living right up among the actual fighting soldiers, miles from any hospital? It had never been done, and therefore, of course, it was useless to try it—so argued the official mind. The other members of the Corps had had the same experiences as Gipsy, but though they saw they did not perceive as she did.

Yet Gipsy never wavered for one moment in her determination. She had the sense and foresight to see that in this original idea lay a field of mighty usefulness; she had the courage to look out over the edge of the rut of custom and convention. She knew instinctively where her own strength lay; she could put through a big thing where others might fail. Opposition only hardened her determination. She began to piece out this great idea, to fit it together. Practical points must be considered. In the first place, she could not run the *poste* herself, and who so suitable to help her as Mairi, the brave little assistant who had been her right hand all along? It was not because Mairi had been her friend in that far-away, almost forgotten life in England that she chose her, but because she had proved herself the possessor of the right kind of qualities, and in spite of her age had a steadiness far removed from that excitable feminine love of rushing about which many women think displays their enthusiasm. It was tolerably certain that she and Mairi together could do more for the lives of the Belgian soldiers than had heretofore been done by all the ambulances together.

A night or two later (November 7) Furnes was shelled in earnest, forty or fifty shells falling into the town. Gipsy and Mairi were still in their disused house, and slept peacefully through it all. One doctor, who occupied the room above them, had a cheerful habit of walking

81

about on the parquet flooring in his thick boots at unearthly hours, so when Gipsy heard of the shelling she expressed surprise at not having been wakened by it; but added: "Though, to be sure, I should never have known the difference between the shells and the doctor's boots, even if I had!" So are the small, near things and the great, far-away things merged into one size by our human limitations.

As the German advance seemed imminent, the time was ripe for the new experiment, and the place chosen must, of course, be approved by the military authorities. Dr. Van der Ghinst was himself now established at Pervyse, which he considered suitable. A road from Dixmude runs westward, and bifurcates at Pervyse. From here the roads form a sort of isosceles triangle, with the base on the sea-coast, one branch running through Furnes and the other to Nieuport. Pervyse therefore lies roughly about half-way between Dixmude and either Furnes or Nieuport. Gipsy, who never let go of anything which she had determined to carry through, one day took out Dr. Van der Ghinst in a car to Pervyse to survey the place and to consider its suitability.

It was obvious that this part of the country was being bludgeoned to death. A week earlier there had been some houses still standing at the sides of the road, but now there was little, not even an upright ruin, only heaps of stones; while the road, which had once boasted a shell-pit here and there, was now pock-marked with them, converted into black cauldrons filled with water by the incessant rain. Driving a car resolved itself into a perpetual gamble, with the odds against one.

All along the road were abandoned motor-cars dashed to pieces even as they ran along, or smashed by a collision with a heavier waggon, which had sent them hurtling into the deep ditch. The prodigal waste of it all was appalling! There was plenty of evidence that the passengers had not always escaped the fate of the cars. In one of them the charred body of the chauffeur was mixed up in grisly fashion with the wrenched and distorted wheel. The air was tainted by the revolting charnel smell, not to be imagined by those who have not experienced it, nor to be forgotten by those who have. The first challenge of it is unmistakable, carrying certainty as to its origin, and it seems to curdle the very blood with its loathsomeness.

Bloated cows like inflated balloons, humped sheep, and horses looking terribly clumsy in grotesque attitudes, lay in the fields; and when they drove into Pervyse, Gipsy exclaimed with conviction: "There is not a house one could even pig it in!"

She little foresaw how long it would be her home!

Dr. Van der Ghinst promised to look out and find, if possible, a shelter for her head among the ruined houses. He advised her, however, to take a rest and go over to England before starting on this new work, as she and Mairi had now been under almost continuous strain, in very trying conditions, for over six weeks. She agreed, and resolved to arrange it. When she returned to the house in Furnes, which she had now grown to look upon as quite her own, to tell her comrade and pack a few clothes, she found Mairi standing speechless before a furiously enraged *bonne*, who was pouring out upon her, in the dialect of her particular native part of France, what she thought of thieves and robbers in general, and of these Two in particular.

Even Gipsy's French, which was better than the average Englishwoman's, was unequal to the situation. The woman flew at them like a hornet, and refused to admit them. She had cautiously returned to collect some clothes for her mistress, and the first glad surprise at finding Furnes still standing, had turned to wrath in her frugal soul when she found evidences of occupation; and they were bound to admit that she was not unjustified from her point of view. They had to fetch the Belgian on whose authority they had established themselves, to explain and set matters right before they could collect their things.

Then away to that glad, strange England, which seemed almost like a foreign country after such amazing experiences. It is hardly to be wondered at that fair-haired Mairi, in her well-worn khaki and knitted soldier's cap, carrying part of a *Uhlan's* lance given to her as a trophy, created quite a sensation in Waterloo Station.

CHAPTER 9

The Cellar-House

By the third week in November, 1914, the Two were established in Pervyse.

A vast area of flood-water, lying flat and white in the cold light, covered acres upon acres of submerged land north of a line between Nieuport and Dixmude. The Belgians had opened the sea-sluices, and those salt waters which had ever lapped hungrily at their small country now proved a strength and protection in enabling them to keep at bay a far more dangerous foe. Reaching up to the margin of the water was a hideous huddle of gaunt stone houses which had once been the peaceful little village of Pervyse.

Gipsy had said with decision that there was not a house to lodge in, and she was right; but there was a cellar—two, in fact—and in one of these the two friends were domiciled for living and sleeping both. It was reached by a rough stairway leading from the battered shell above, which had once been the house it belonged to. The dim project had taken shape.

When the two friends had returned to their work after being a few days in England, unfortunate Mairi had been taken ill, and was unable to go at once to the cellar-house; but now she was all right again, and they were installed in surely the very oddest circumstances two women had ever managed to get themselves into before. In the other remaining cellar across the road were the officers of the Mitrailleuse Third Division, to which Dr. Van der Ghinst was attached.

To get a clear idea of Pervyse, it is necessary to enter it from the direction of Furnes, where the road makes several curves, and at the last goes quite straight and gives evidence that it comes well within the range of the German shells. The village which once lay along the sides of this road was rather like a Scotch village, for the houses were built of stone, and stood right on to the edge of the road, so they had that bare, unfinished appearance which is so disappointing to the stranger first visiting Scotland, who is accustomed to the bright little flower-gardens of the south-country villages of England. Every one of these houses had been smashed up by the continual rain of missiles. Houses without man are the most melancholy sight, it is the soul without the body, though, oddly enough, it is when they are broken up that they bear most resemblance to the body, showing a series of distorted faces.

At the top of the village stood the church, which had originally had a dumpy spire; but the top of this had been shot away, so that it was left square. Of this church the late Miss Macnaughtan wrote:

"A haggard-looking church, like a sentinel with both eyes shot out. Nothing was left but a blind face. The tower had great holes in it, and the aisles had fallen. The churchyard looked as though some devil had stalked through it tearing up crosses and digging up graves."

This churchyard is as thickly crowded with bodies as the old London city churchyards before they were cleared out. Not only Belgians, but hundreds of Germans have been buried there. The remnants of tombstones had been hurled this way and that, graves gaped, giving up their dead, and the scrubby trees were withered and stripped by the fiery blasts. The two cellars were at the church end of the village, the dangerous end, nearest to the German guns. Water was scarce, and when they first went there the Two had to use the flood-water in the ditch, so it is probably true, as one paper remarked, that they drank water which had filtered down from the graveyard, where lay scores of dead Germans!

At right angles to the main road run both the railway line and the Nieuport-Dixmude road, which crosses the other just on the Pervyse side of the line, and all along by the railway line are the Belgian trenches commanding the flooded area beyond. It must be remembered that in Belgian flood-areas trenches are not exactly what one usually understands by that term. Instead of being "dug-outs," they are "throw-ups." It would be obviously impossible in that saturated soil to make any trench which did not immediately become a ditch, and therefore earth-works are thrown up, which serve the same purpose, and even then the men are most of their time in water, in spite of much pumping. Many of them constantly trudged through the village carrying great bundles of straw, which they threw down to give them for a short time a dry standing space. Their little shelters are built along by the earth-work, then roofed over and filled with straw, and at night comes a faint glow through the insufficient roofs, telling of dim lights and smoky fires within, where the men lie huddled upon their primitive cribs.

The Furnes road does not end at the line, but goes on across it, and runs out into the great waste of water like a pointing finger. It is raised, as nearly all main Belgian roads are, and forms a sort of pier or bund, so has to be strongly guarded. The Belgian outposts are established far out upon it. Behind the wide belt of water is still preserved the "very small remnant" of their fertile land left to King and people; small as it is, it forms a well-spring of hope and good omen for the future.

The blessed belt encircling such a priceless territory is comparatively shallow, but very unequal in depth, and therein lies its value. Even if the German infantry could start knee-deep to march across it, they might any minute find themselves up to their necks in ditch or hole, and at the best the heavy guns of the artillery would stick in the plastic paste beneath. In the shroud of the shallow grey water are buried German guns which had to be left in the headlong flight when the sluices were opened, and the invaders fled pell-mell, to escape the fate which overtook so many. An uncertain grey hump floating here and there suggesting a water-turtle, betrays the drowned bodies. Simple as it seems, this stretch of shallow water is at once the slightest and most permanent barrier that could be found. On that grey November day, when Gipsy and Mairi wandered out to get some idea of their surroundings, great bars of yellow drifted through the pervading fog, and made spots of colour on the water, where the dead fish, killed by the effects of the salt water, were floating dismally, with their white undersides turned to the sky.

The sides of that raised road were sprinkled with dead animals. Twenty-seven cows, five sheep, eight pigs, and three horses could be counted before the outpost was reached. Standing on the Belgian side, and looking out from an observation-post across the water, it seemed like a shallow sea, broken here and there by islands. On one of them was a picturesque ruin which had once been a pleasant *chateau*; on another, nearer, was a farmhouse in a clump of trees. It was not often that the moisture-laden atmosphere permitted a glimpse of the far side, but when it could be seen it showed itself as a low line of trees, behind which were the German guns, from which ever and again at stated times tongues of fire belched forth and missiles leaped across the water, sometimes falling short of their objective and generating huge geysers, sometimes pitching well into the village, and with a thunderous roar shattering into a heap one more of the tottering walls.

It was here the Two settled down in a crumbling house, with every pane of glass shattered to splinters and the walls gaping. A musty smell of the dust of ancient bricks and mortar, compounded with dirt and damp, hung over it all. There was no comfort, no convenience of any kind. To have to sleep there one night would have been considered a hardship by most people. The light was always dim, for the cellar was lit only by gratings in the pavement above. It was, perhaps, ten feet by about twelve feet, and so low that Gipsy, who is not much above medium height, could just stand upright in it. Mairi, of course, found plenty of space for her lesser inches, also it suited most of the little Belgian soldiers well enough, but there came a day when a King —— But that must be told in its own place!

Yet they set to work at once to make it cheery. They marked it outside by a Union Jack and the Belgian and French flags, and it was not long before they were joined by the Lion of Scotland, for a Scot is never so Scottish as when away from his, or her, own land.

The first need was some sort of a fire to cook by. They found a stove, which they humoured like the family cat, for it had all the attributes of that animal, taking everything for granted and immovably refusing to do what was required of it in return, and behaving generally as if the cellar had been built for its convenience. Two soldiers had been sleeping in the cellar on some straw when the new tenants arrived. They were good, willing lads, called Alphonse and Desiré, and they at once set themselves to be useful, and helped to loot a few necessary bits of furniture from the deserted houses round. When all was done there was not very much; a table, a few chairs, and some straw held in its place by a board, were the principal items, and even then there was hardly room to move. Here the Two settled down. At night they lay down as they were in their clothes; as Mairi explains, "To dress, that means to brush one's hair and put on one's boots."

They were seldom alone; the Cockney chauffeur, Woffington, slept in one corner, and the little cook, Alexandre, in another. This was of necessity also, for the cellar was the only place in Pervyse which provided even a measure of safety from the shells. If other members of the ambulance party turned up, as they sometimes did, they generally went back to Fumes the same day, but if any of them stayed they had to sleep there too. The first night the American lady and Dr, Van der Ghinst were both there. How they all fitted in is a puzzle. Certainly

THE MAIN STREET OF PERVYSE AS IT WAS.

THE MAIN STREET OF PERVYSE AS IT IS.

THE CELLAR-HOUSE, PERVYSE
(INSET ALEXANDRE THE COOK).

THE CELLAR-HOUSE FROM THE BACK

one could not have set a boot on the ground between them.

The details of settling in and finding household requisites were work after Mairi's own heart. She was never so satisfied as when she was giving everything a "good turn-out" and making all comfortable! Aided by some of the Belgian Engineer officers, quartered in a ruined house at the other end of the village, she climbed by means of a plank over to a farmhouse on an island which had been left desolate. Here they found spoons, forks, plates, knives, and other necessaries. A few cabbages and potatoes might still be scraped up in the gardens and patches of ground, and these were most welcome for the soldiers' soup. A little lean-to outhouse, in which there was, most fortunately, a copper in working order, had been made into a kitchen, and here the soup for the weary, frozen men in the trenches was made.

Alexandre, the cook, was a cheery little Belgian lad of seventeen; he had a bullet head and a *serio*-comic expression that made one laugh to look at him. He had been through all the fighting, and considered this relegation to the kitchen as a "soft thing." He had an immense sense of his own importance, and very quickly let people know that, in spite of his lack of inches and years, he was master of his own quarter-deck; even the officers who hung around, drawn by the savoury whiffs that came forth, were quickly sent about their business. Alexandre was no longer a private, but a chef! It was the difference between an ordinary seaman in the Navy and the captain of a merchant ship. He soon became known far and wide as "*le magnifique petit cuisinier.*" He and the other two worked of their own accord, for at this time the military authorities gave no countenance to this astounding project.

Alphonse and Desiré were Walloons, and manifested all the striking divergencies which lie between Walloon and Fleming, countrymen though they be. The Walloon is excitable, talkative, and inclined to be frivolous. It is true that when he works he generally puts his whole heart into it, but he is only too ready to knock off and have a chat with anyone who will oblige him. He is very intelligent and fond of mechanical inventions; he readily grasps the idea of new machinery, and makes a good chauffeur. He has a great deal in common with the Frenchman, which is hardly wonderful. Youth seems his most characteristic feature; the simplest things amuse him, and he runs eagerly, like the Athenians, after "any new thing."

He is up and down, extravagant, careless, attractive—all by turns. He wins your heart and hurts you, and brings you round again, so that you forgive him and would do anything for him; but you are left with a conviction, after all, that he does not much care. It is hardly to be supposed that with all this the Walloon is going to submit easily to discipline, and as most of the chauffeurs which the Two had from time to time were Walloons, there was frequent trouble. As Mairi explains, "If you say to him, 'Do that,' he will immediately not do it! If you say, 'Will you please do that?' he will think about it. You must lead them, not drive them, or you'll never get a thing done." About their courage, however, there cannot be two opinions. And it was something to have a couple of men who could do heavy lifting when it got beyond women's strength.

The atmosphere in the cellar naturally got a little dense after a night, and it was very early in the morning when Gipsy climbed the ladder, and, putting her head out, indulged in a long indrawn breath of the sharp morning air. It was keenly cold, everything was frozen hard, and the white cat-ice snapped on the puddles in the road. She had hardly been there a second when she was joined by Mairi.

At first it was very difficult to get accustomed to the perpetual feeling of dirt and being tumbled. After a day or two camping out anyone knows how "lived in" one's clothes feel; but the clean, natural surroundings of woods are Paradise compared with a dank cellar. The sense of discomfort was very great, but there was nothing for it but to grin and bear it; and there was so much to do, it was forgotten after a while. The very first morning job was to see that Alexandre did his duty in getting the fire under the copper alight and the appetizing soup heated. It was soon bubbling away, with cabbage, turnips, and potatoes and other ingredients in, and was poured out still scalding hot into pans, which the orderlies carried to the trenches, following the Two. The trenches were only fifty yards away, and the men who had been on watch or trying to sleep in their icy little shelters, insufficiently clad, were thankful to see this vision of Paradise, and greeted these wonderful English ladies with enthusiasm, holding out their little mugs in stiff, frozen fingers. Oh, the joy of being able to do it! It was worthwhile to have gone through all the weary days of waiting and the disagreeables for this! But, alas! though there seemed quantities of soup when they started, it was never enough—they could have done with much more.

The difficulty of dealing it out into the small mugs was considerable, and the Two usually came back to their own breakfast splashed with soup but glowing with pleasure.

In the days that followed, the grand success of the soup was almost eclipsed by the charms of the chocolate which succeeded it later in the day. Cauldron after cauldron of this was emptied as quickly as it could be made. When the men were relieved in the trenches they came over to the little cellar-house, and swarmed around it like bees, waiting patiently for their turn, and holding out those endless mugs which became like a nightmare to the fillers. Hour after hour chocolate was scooped up and poured in, and the stains of dirty brown formed a pattern with the stains of greasy soup on the khaki suits of the two patient workers, whose backs ached after this really hard manual toil. Yet there was nowhere to rest; it was impossible, even had there been time, to go and lie down on the dank straw in the cellar, with people coming in and out, and there was nowhere else to go.

What the perpetual dirt and cold and discomfort meant to these Two can hardly be put into words. There was no privacy and no possibility of a good wash: their hands quickly became engrained with scrubbing, potato-peeling, and other rough work. To keep the place habitable at all, with the continual incursion of wet and wounded men, was difficult. To get rid of soiled, stained bandages was difficult. There was a constant smell of disinfectants and stagnant or rotting things. Continual wet penetrated everywhere, and in those early days they had not learned, as they did later, the best way to equip themselves against this.

The news of this extraordinary little centre of light and comfort right up in the actual firing-line spread like wild-fire, and every Belgian officer discovered that urgent business took him to Pervyse at one time or another in the next few weeks. They appreciated the chocolate just as much as the soldiers did, and also the English way of making tea, "the four o'clock," and the tiny cellar was generally packed about that hour, while Mairi, with a flushed face, hastened to and fro, wondering if the supply would last out for all these guests. The very fact that the ladies were there in the midst of them, English ladies, backing them up and believing in them, sent the spirits of the whole division up degrees higher. It was the 9th Regiment that was then stationed at Pervyse, and they began to look upon the ladies as their particular property, and crowed over the other unfortunates who had no such luck.

In the ruin of the house above the cellar was a half-buried piano, and one day one of the officers, being unable at that moment to squeeze into the cellar, try he never so hard, cleared away the stones and rubbish that had fallen on it, and discovered that though it missed a part of the keyboard in the treble, the rest went all right, so he sat down and played a waltz to fill up the time. Immediately those of the rank and file who were hanging about outside started dancing, their heavy boots clashing on the frosty road, until the party in the cellar emerged to see what was going on. As the ladder disgorged man after man it seemed a miracle where so many had managed to pack themselves. Mairi, flourishing the immense kitchen spoon with which the soup was stirred, beat time for the dancers. The rattling piano, with its occasional lapses, wheezed gaily away in the wind-swept ruin, the ruddy-faced men and the two handsome women laughed helplessly, while the hidden death waited ready to pounce. It was like laughing in a lions' den; it was all right for the moment, but anything might happen.

A strange life, indeed!

There was even a worse job to be faced than that of carrying the soup to the trenches in the morning. This was to visit the sentries and outposts at night, over the railway line, towards l'Yser, and carry the warm comfort to feed their bodies, and the cheery thought, they were remembered, to brace up their minds.

After tea this hung ominously over the girls; it was the worst bit of the day, but it had to be faced. It could not be done until it got dark, and then, as often as not, the shelling began. So they took their lives in their hands, and never knew when they started out if they would come back.

They were always accompanied by an officer, who had the password, and the mission had to be carried out in perfect silence, so as not to attract the enemy's unwelcome attentions. Sometimes there was a gleam from the stars if it were frosty, but generally, frosty or not, the damp from the ground rose in a white winding-sheet and shut out all such light. Their feet rang on the iron-bound road in spite of all their care; they carried the heavy jugs of scalding liquid, and the sudden challenge, "*Halte là!*" ringing out in the night, always made them jump, though they knew, or perhaps because they knew, it would come.

"*Officier Belge,*" was the reply.

"*Un homme en avance,*" commanded the voice of the unseen sentry, and the officer moved slowly forward within five paces of him, while the others waited till the password and countersign had been softly given and received.

Three times this ceremony had to be repeated as they went out

The men in the "Trenches"

Some of the Belgian Soldiers,

DESOLATION

THE HOUSES FROM THE BACK.

and three times on their return, but on the outward journey each grateful sentry received a cup of hot chocolate as a delightful reward.

Out across the bleak raised road, with the water lapping at its sides, or with the thin crackle of ice settling down, they went. There was a pale line of radiance from their own side where the trenches lay, and sometimes the flashes of the German artillery shone out across the water, or occasionally a star-shell, making a radiance more glorious than the heart of the lightning. Then they had to catch their steps at once and stand still as stocks, jug in hand, until the star burst and faded. The air was full of portent and menace. Once as a doctor advanced on this very road to meet Gipsy a shell caught him, so that he died. "Why was it he, and not I ?" Any sensitive mind must ask that question.

The men of the *mitrailleuse* who guarded the outpost lived in a hole in the ground. In pitch darkness a hand groped for the jug and drew it in, and then, their work accomplished, the little party started back again on their eerie journey.

Back across the railway line night after night, with the woolly fog touching damp faces like unearthly fingers, then goodnight to the officer, and the stumble down into the little "cave," where the stove was perhaps giving off a warm glow, reflected on the red blankets and the slumbering form of Woffington. They crawled into their sleeping-sacks, and slept the dead sleep of those whose whole being has endured to the utmost during the run of daylight.

CHAPTER 10

Varied Life in Pervyse

In any society in the world two such attractive women would excite a good deal of admiration, but out here, where the raw edge of life was so apparent and recreation of any sort was so scarce, they shone brilliantly. Gipsy is by nature very outspoken, and in her dealings with headquarters she had made everyone she met understand very clearly just what she wanted and how it was to be done, and done it generally was. Her excessive frankness did not always make for friendship, and some people were even offended by her outspokenness. She was so quick and efficient herself that she had not much of that patience which "*suffers fools gladly,*" though she could be patience itself with suffering.

Like all natures which have a touch, or more than a touch, of genius in them, she was very original, up and down, and full of facets, showing first one side and then another, until some people thought they would never be able to understand her. Her stern determination to get through against opposition, her rapier strokes at those who stood in the way, showed an entirely different side of her character from that she displayed in off-times, when she was as much a child as the best Belgian among them. She threw off cares and concentrated herself entirely on the moment, and being an excellent mimic and very versatile, she could entertain anyone until they too forgot the sadness of the world around and were completely absorbed in her.

The wonderful position in which she found herself had been entirely due to her own brilliant idea and quick grasp of what was necessary in the first instance, and her wonderful perseverance in the second; she never spared herself, and never rested till she had put through what she had set her mind on. But she hated detail; in developing the large outline of a scheme lay her strength—the detail must be carried out by others. Like many another of the same temperament, she "could not be bothered with small businesses," as the Indian fortune-teller said. She needed someone behind who would pick up what she dropped and see that she did not kill herself with excess of energy, and Mairi was exactly the person required. Mairi is eminently sane and steady. She cannot bear to sit down in an untidy room; she must know where to lay hands on anything that might be needed at a moment's notice; she is free from any trace of egotism, and has a large capacity for hero-worship, yet, withal, the shrewdness not to offer it at unworthy shrines. She is keen, competent, and trustworthy, and the two together at Pervyse made a perfect combination.

The officers who surrounded them adored them, as was only natural, and were equally divided in their admiration of "*Madame*" and "Miss."

Dr. Van der Ghinst, through whose frank cheeriness there ran a deeper undercurrent of observation and perception, was a constant friend and adviser. He very nearly fulfilled the highest ideal of manhood, one who could have bestowed the most patient attention on the wounded finger of someone else, even though he himself was bleeding to death from something much more serious. Since the Two had arrived in Pervyse, he had always been ready to listen and to enter into any plan for the welfare and comfort of the soldiers. He was an unfailing inspiration in the work. He was more fortunate than many, for his wife was safe, and even paid a visit to Pervyse.

Another of the Belgian officers of whom the Two had seen a good deal in Furnes was Captain Robert de Wilde, and when he turned up and became observation officer in Pervyse they were delighted. He was a perfect companion; "he never needed entertaining, but it always seemed it was just right for him to be there." What higher tribute could mortal man desire?

He got into the way of dropping in most evenings, and then there was patience, or jigsaw puzzles, or, best of all, discussions on those deep questions which must lie below the surface in the hearts of all thoughtful men and women, and which are revealed at times when the bare facts of human existence lie starkly uncovered and all spurious sentiment falls away. These discussions meant much to Gipsy, who needed mental stimulation; they left both her and Mairi refreshed and brightened. "The nearer to the trenches, the gayer we are!" she exclaimed one day, and indeed, it is not only at Pervyse this truth is apparent. It is in the intervals of great crises that men let themselves go with light-heartedness; the heights are proportionate to the depths.

Into no humdrum life has ever entered the utter abandonment of gaiety felt at times by those who have faced incredible danger and hardship. All happiness lies in contrast.

One morning Gipsy was alone in the cellar for a marvel; she was reading a very dirty old magazine in a rare interval of leisure, for there was no call for her services. Someone knocked and came slowly down the steps. She saw in a moment, in spite of the dim light, that this was a newcomer, and not any of the officers she had yet met. He was very tall, so tall that he could not stand upright in the cellar, though he tried more than once; and he wore the smart uniform of the Guides, with crimson breeches, shining boots, green tunic, and peaked cap. Somehow she felt unaccountably embarrassed, and suddenly aware that she was in soiled clothes, sitting on a heap of straw in a most unbecoming way. What was it in the presence of this young man—he was only a lieutenant—that should shed such a brilliant illumination on things? It was very remarkable, and she felt inclined to laugh, not knowing that with him had entered her Fate!

Courteously saluting, he handed her a message from his colonel, and turned to retrace his steps; and as he went he smiled, a smile that lit up his face and indeed the whole cellar. That smile seemed positively to linger and irradiate everything in a remarkable way!

She felt unusually shy about mentioning the incident to Mairi, and it was not until they passed him one day on his way to the trenches, when he smiled again as he saluted, and Mairi asked casually, "Who's that?" that Gipsy owned having met him at all.

"I don't know his name; he came with a message from the colonel," she said, and felt, to her dismay, that she was growing very red as she spoke.

It was less than a week after that the young lieutenant once again appeared, this time bearing a box of *marrons glacés* as a present from the colonel. A very welcome sight it was, for they both loved sweets; indeed, Gipsy once plaintively remarks in one of her home letters, "There is no more chocolate in the whole of Belgium, and none in Dunkirk, so I feel horribly lonely."

Whether it was the *marrons glacés* or the smile she could not tell, but from that date she had a feeling of security and comfort so long as the young Lieutenant was in the trenches, though they saw very little of him. Pervyse seemed in a miraculous way to have become a safe and singularly happy place. And when, a couple of months later he was suddenly transferred elsewhere, and went without a goodbye, though she saw him march off, it seemed as if the whole side of Pervyse had been laid bare, and the Germans might sweep in at any moment!

One day a little later she found it impossible to get a necessary matter attended to. "I will go myself, and speak to Headquarters about it," she said; "it's the only way to get anything done." So she mounted her motor-cycle and went off, intending to let Headquarters see how very unpleasant she could make herself when they would not attend to her wishes. She had been feeling like that lately, as if she rather wanted to blow someone up. "Nerves," she called it to herself.

Now as she ran out on the long, raised road she had to stop for a moment to attend to her cycle, and a car which was careering along from the opposite direction stopped just beside her while the occupants showed the sentries their papers. With a start which thrilled right through her, Gipsy saw that young Lieutenant de T'Serclaes, whose name she had now learned, was in the car, and that he was in a new uniform with the wings of an aviator on his sleeve. Again that happy smile seemed to strike through her, but no word passed between them. She mounted her cycle, and involuntarily looked back as the car spun on its way. It was a most curious coincidence, but the lieutenant looked back too, at precisely the same moment! Somehow the feeling of annoyance and "nerves" fell from Gipsy; she suddenly felt herself again, and noticed how the larks were singing in the battered fields around! She changed her mind, after all; she wasn't going to bully Headquarters, she didn't feel she wanted to bully anyone to-day, and she rode back again to Pervyse in a state of serene bliss.

Supplying soup and chocolate was not the whole reason for the settlement at Pervyse, or indeed the chief one—there were casualties to be attended to and much suffering saved. The word "casualties" by no means implies only actual wounds caused by weapons, but all those terrible hurts due to the exposure of men's bodies in circumstances of hard-ship and want. The intense cold and the lack of proper clothing had their share in bringing about misery and suffering, which in a minor degree, but still quite appreciably, affected the fighting power of Belgium. Bare toes met the frost through burst boots, and pneumonia and bronchitis supervened upon nights of shivering, soaked bodies.

Gipsy wrote home urgently for clothes, clothes of any description; they were not particular. At that time the Belgian Army was not clad in khaki, and the soldiers were ready enough to snatch up any warm garment they could find; a motley crowd they looked sometimes, but they were units whose individualism would have stood a stronger test than a lack of uniformity in garments, which might have imperilled the cohesion of a German regiment. "I wish I could get hold of some society that has heaps and heaps of soldiers' clothing," Gipsy says. "Helmets, scarves, boots, and socks."

From the first the *poste* was on an organized and systematic footing. There were to be no casual loiterers playing at stomach-ache to secure the comforts it offered; every man who came to ask for the ladies' assistance had to bring a letter from his commanding officer warranting that he was in need of it.

Such varying needs, too! One had caught his hand on a nail, and the wound was festering; another was in agony with swollen, inflamed feet; a third was quite done up, nothing to show except that he was incapable of the smallest exertion. Him they fed and put into what they called the "*blessé*" bed "in the corner, because it was devoted to the soldiers. They piled up hot-water bottles round him, and let him sleep the clock round, after which he arose a new man.

Every morning one or other of the Two was up at six to see Alexandre did not neglect his duties in getting the fire alight. Mairi sometimes went foraging, and though she generally started alone, she was seldom allowed to return so. To the Belgian officers her roguish smile and the dimple in her sweet face were like sunlight, and she never lacked admirers, but through them all she passed unscathed. Her heart was not easy to reach. She was charming to all, with a frank independence that was like that of a delightful boy, and was new to most of them in a woman. She made use of them and listened to their chaff or their compliments with just the same manner, and the humour she shared in common with most of her countrymen, despite the gross libel kept alive by those who wouldn't know a Scot if they met one, was constantly in play. Her nerve was unassailable; she went to dig up potatoes and came back laden through a shower of shrapnel, which she apparently regarded much as she would a shower of rain.

Here is an account of one such incident in her own words:

We found some potatoes up the road past the trenches. Then we went right to the other side of the village to get some cabbages. When we had cut them we wanted to wash them, and were shown a well. This done, we started back. Just behind the church we were warned it was impossible to get back, as the Germans were plumping shrapnel across the road. We decided to take our chance, so went on. Immediately the shrapnel came whistling along and burst just over us, so we ducked in under a house. Then we went on again and got in safely. The shrapnel continued all the morning.

And with this life, so full and rich in the most life-giving element of all, the knowledge that one's presence is almost indispensable to the well-being and happiness of many, a great peace descended on the Two. Shell-fire, the desolation of that curved street with gaping wounds, and the lack of all amenities, had not power to affect them. They quickly grew to love their little cellar-house, and to feel that it was a true home.

One morning they awoke to a perfect fusillade of rifle-fire, and for the first grave moment thought the Germans had really broken through and were charging up the village street. They climbed up out of their shelter and gazed down the street, for, as Gipsy said, "Curiosity beat fear." They saw no Germans, so they scampered along in the direction of the trenches, determined at all costs to satisfy their curiosity, and there they met a dismal procession. One or two men were being helped along as they stumbled and stayed, leaving heavy red drops on the road; others were being carried on stretchers; and the cause was that one of the trenches had caught fire, and a quantity of ammunition had given a demonstration on its own account, with the result that no less than six soldiers suffered. They were tenderly cared for, for by this time Mairi was a most efficient assistant, far better after her practical experience than many who have spent months in bandaging imaginary patients. But all this was done under great difficulties.

There was no clean running water; no sinks and other appliances—only a dim, dark cellar, so small that one could hardly turn round; no room to store anything; constant curtailment of everything that a medical man would have looked upon as indispensable. The shortage of water was a great bother. There had been numerous pumps and wells, but most of them were choked or smashed. It was a great triumph when the genius Alexandre, poking about by himself in the dusty heaps of bricks and great fallen beams that now represented Pervyse, actually discovered a pump in working order. With that phlegm which was his most valuable quality, he annexed the top part of the pump, so that no one else could use it, and so exhaust the supply. As water even for drinking or cooking purposes was scarce, it may be deduced that water for baths was unobtainable.

It was so at first, and as the Two slept night after night in their clothes—a proceeding which exhausts a woman far more than a man—a bath became a thing to sigh for. Of all the luxuries in England, the wide rooms, the dainty food and accessories, the soft sheets, the thought of a hot bath was the most alluring. The best they could do was to get a bucket of hot water occasionally, but the difficulty was to know when to make use of it, for the cellar-house was never free from intrusion any moment, night or day. It might be that Mairi had stationed herself on the topmost rung of the ladder to scare away all comers while Gipsy had a delicious wash below; but who was to foretell whether at that very moment when the bather was most helpless before convention, a desperate wounded man needing immediate succour might not materialize?

At last a bath was discovered, a real porcelain bath of the latest kind—a most unusual thing to be in a Belgian village at all. It was unearthed in one of the tumble-down houses, and carted bodily into one of the ruined rooms above the cellar, where, by disregarding the risk of being shelled at any minute, one could have a bath with the strictly minimum amount of privacy necessary for decency. But before this great find was made Gipsy, getting desperate, borrowed a beautiful horse belonging to one of the officers and rode into L'Espérance, the little place where Dr. Van der Ghinst and other officers were now quartered, where was a tiny inn and the possibility of a wholesale wash. Just as she arrived there she met an Englishman. She looked at him keenly and he at her, and for a moment they paused, not knowing whether the flash of familiarity that passed between them was merely due to the magnetic attraction of a country-man and woman in a strange land, or the result of real acquaintance somewhere in that old, almost-forgotten life lived once, centuries ago, before the war. Gipsy recovered first, as the woman invariably does. She leaned down over her horse's silky neck, and said softly: "It was hard luck that you couldn't manage that last rise at Leith Hill! You would have beaten me!"

Quick as a flash the newcomer retorted, laughing, "My own fault for having let the beastly thing leak; all the petrol had run out." Then they plunged into delightful reminiscences of the day of the motor-cycle contest and hill-climbing test, but all at once Gipsy sat up straight, and her delicate eyebrows drew together with an expression of anxiety as she looked back the way she had come.

"Firing," he said, following her glance. "They say the Boches are shelling Pervyse."

MAIRI BESIDE A SHELL HOLE.

ANOTHER SORT OF SHELL-HOLE.

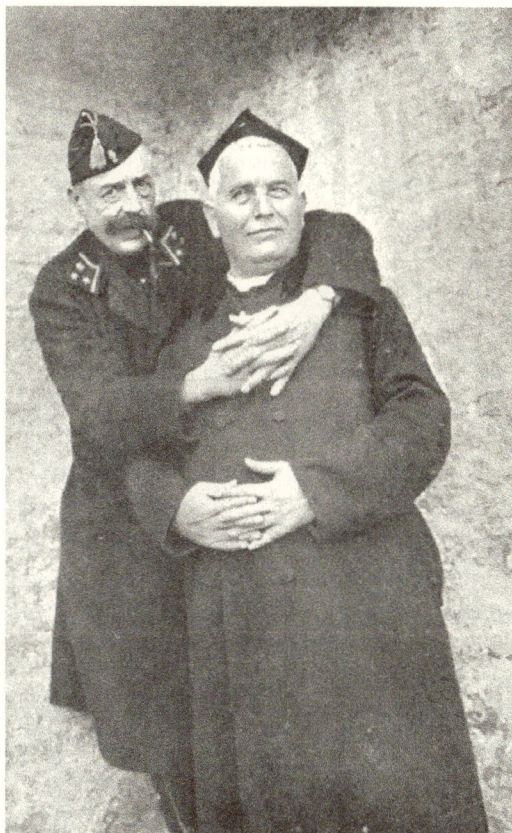

ARMS AND THE PRIEST.

"Pervyse !" She sat straighter. "Oh yes, a few shells, Pervyse often gets those, but this is a storm !"

"So they say," he answered, waving indifferently toward two officers who had come out and were standing at the entrance of the inn.

"I must go back instantly." All thoughts of her bath were merged in the remembrance that Mairi was there alone in that tornado, far worse than anything they had yet been subjected to at the *poste*.

The Englishman caught her rein. "Go back? Good lord! Why? You're well out of it!"

She only laughed, flicked her rein from his hand, and with a cool nod trotted off hard toward the ominous sound. Dismounting on the outskirts of Pervyse, she hitched the horse up in one of the broken-down barns and went on on foot. But the firing was terrific. Shells began to burst around, and involuntarily she sprang to the meagre shelter of some broken walls. Then Woffington came round the corner driving a car as hard as he could go, with that curious silence they had already noticed, which made it seem like an object in a cinematograph. She stepped out and shouted to him to stop, and Woffington, who always had his wits about him, obeyed coolly. He said Miss Chisholm had sent him post-haste for the doctor, as a lot of wounded had been brought in. However, he turned without cavil and carried Mrs. Knocker back into the deadly fire-zone, setting her down at the cellar, before once more he reversed his car and ran out on his errand; and to his credit it may be noted his hand did not shake, nor had his colour in any way abated.

The wounded were, as he had said, crowded in the cellar, with Mairi and the old priest kneeling by them; there was hardly room to get in beside them. One of the men over whom Gipsy bent had had his arm nearly severed, and with a quick contraction of the heart she recollected having met him on his way to the trenches as she rode out to L'Espérance only an hour before. *Then* he had given her a royal salute, and now never again would he be able to salute with that poor arm.

After hard work, the wounded were patched up sufficiently to be sent down to Furnes.

A day or so before this they had had a great excitement, for word had come that King Albert, the hero-King whom they were serving, was in the village. He did not come to the cellar, for which they were thankful, as he is so very tall. Mairi was certain he would have bumped his head "every minute," which would have been awful; but he spoke kindly to them both, with that absence of conventionality which characterizes him.

With all the stern, and many times ghastly, scenes that they went through, there were bright intervals of enjoyment that stood out like beacons by the way. One of these was when an invitation came from the Engineer officers stationed at the bottom of the village for the two British ladies to go to dinner with them. They had lived so sparsely and simply on biscuits, chocolate, bully-beef, and cheese, and spent so little time or thought on preparing their own meals, that this came as a glad surprise. They had not realized until then how tired they were of the coarse, monotonous fare. They spent a whole hour beforehand trying to work themselves up to a due standard of attractiveness for the great occasion; but some stains on their worn clothes were impossible to remove. Exactly at six o'clock, as arranged, a couple of officers came to escort them on foot, and they passed down that wide, curved street, with the rows of shattered houses and the heaps of barbed wire, among which were one or two scanty, leafless trees sticking up perkily, not yet splintered or blasted by the firing.

The officers were waiting to greet them with *éclat*. The house in which they were quartered was in better condition than most of the others in the village, and they had made it still more habitable. A round table was set out in the middle, though their utmost efforts had been unable to produce a cloth! Mairi says, "When the menu was presented to us, we nearly had a fit!" so surprising was the fare. She knew well their hosts must have worked for days beforehand to get such a menu together in this wilderness.

MENU.
Anchois d'Écosse.
Potage tomates.
Asperges Irlandaises.
Pré salé.
Haricots verts.
Poulets.
Petits pois.
Saucisson.
Salade.
Desserts variés.

WINE.
Chateau Grand Puech.
Haut Médoc and Champagne.

"If that isn't fine, I don't know what is!"

But this was not all. Music was also provided, and one of the soldiers, a born musician, played to them Liszt's *Rhapsodies* and other pieces out of his head during dinner, for the officers of the *génie* had also managed to procure a piano.

The Two passed a gay and charming evening, and about 10.30 were safely escorted home again, a very necessary precaution, as the sentries in the village were apt to let off their rifles on very small provocation after dark.

They had hardly got to sleep, feeling well fed and comforted in mind and body, when Gipsy was awakened by stealthy footsteps coming cautiously down the stairs. She turned on the electric torch she carried for emergencies, and, as the door was thrust back, saw two Belgian soldiers carrying another. The poor man was in agony, with a leg smashed by shrapnel and hanging by a thread. It was too bad a case for even a skilful nurse to manage, and, after examining it, she decided to have a doctor. But the chauffeur was away in Furnes, so she had to turn out herself and walk down the village to find the doctor, who slept with the soldiers. He came at once and did what he could willingly and cheerfully, but the poor fellow was too far gone to be saved. There was no more sleep, however, for the soldier's friend, who lay awake and constantly got up to ease him or minister to him as he moved and groaned. He was sent down to the hospital at Furnes the next day, but he died shortly after.

It was quite obvious that, in spite of its advantage in being comparatively safe, the cellar was very unsuitable in many ways for the work, and the picture of that poor wretch with his trailing leg coming down the steep ladder, developed an idea that had been germinating in Gipsy's head. She discussed with Dr. Van der Ghinst and her friends, the Engineer officers, if it were possible to make a room in the house itself—say, on the ground floor—habitable, so that at least it could be used throughout the day and save the brave fellows much pain. The idea was accepted enthusiastically; everything that was feasible should be done at once.

The house outside was just like any little straight up-and-down English cottage. The roof had been broken to pieces, but the passage on the ground floor was weather-tight, and out of this there opened a room on the right that, by a little shoring-up and roofing-in, could be made habitable. This was accomplished without delay, and, when it was finished, Gipsy says with delight, "It was lovely." To her impressionable nature surroundings meant much, and the mere fact of being able to have an open fire and to be above-ground made her very happy.

When the Two moved into this palatial apartment there was a great merry-making. While they were all enjoying themselves, they heard the steady tramp of the "dear little soldiers "outside collecting to replace those who had had their turn in the trenches. There was not a man of them who did not look at the little house, marked by drooping flags, with a softened feeling in his heart, for that battered house to nearly all of them for the moment represented "home." It must be remembered that these men had, in the great majority of cases, lost sight of parents, wives, or children. They did not know if they would ever see them again. They were up against a foe with enormous resources and crushing strength. All their country, except one tiny strip, was in the hands of that enemy; their conditions were most miserable.

They lacked everything. The trenches were sodden and often actually under water, the weather was bitter; yet they were still cheerful, and though not by nature a fighting race, the brutal outrage of their giant neighbour had aroused in them a spirit equal to that of the most dour Scot. Also they had to uphold them the example of their noble King and Queen, whose fortitude is beyond anything that has ever been recorded of Sovereigns. They had never left Belgian soil, and behind them was Britain, which had never yet been beaten. As a sign of it, here were these two British ladies, who had come to share the hardships and dangers of the rough soldiers, and live actually among them, to make for them a little bit of home in the wilderness. Some of these men were really clever in a variety of odd ways. Two of them played well and musically on two lengths of lead piping they had picked up and twisted into shape.

An account of an ordinary day is given by Mairi about this time. "Our job is to get up at six, make chocolate or something hot, and keep it served all the day." No light job, either! From twelve to three some days without ceasing, except to snatch a biscuit, they served out chocolate, and as they had to go out late to the outposts, and were often disturbed in the night, it did not leave much time for rest.

One day, Mairi, coming back with a pail full of potatoes, found a very young lieutenant—a mere infant—standing outside the shattered house, but not daring to set his foot therein. He looked younger than he was, because his hair was of the soft downy kind seen on all very young things. She knew quite well he cherished an adoration for

BELGIAN OFFICERS.

FRIENDS (THE FATHER IN THE CENTRE).

CAPTAIN ROBERT DE WILDE.

PERVYSE
(THE "GÉNIE" HOUSE ON EXTREME RIGHT).

Gipsy so deep that it almost tore him in two, and that his appetite for bully-beef had been so seriously impaired that it had provoked comment. He flushed a pretty pink all over his chubby little face when he saw her, and saluted, but did not move.

"Are you going on duty?" she asked, for Mairi, whose French had been of the schoolroom variety when she arrived, now rushed headlong into it on all occasions.

"*Non, Mamselle.*"

"Are you going off duty?"

"*Non, Mamselle.*"

"Are you going to do anything?"

"*Non, Mamselle.*"

"What are you standing there for, then?"

"*Rien du tout, Mamselle.*"

She burst out laughing and ran into the room. "Oh, you infant-catcher," she addressed the astonished Gipsy, "go and see your handiwork, and think scorn of yourself!"

Gipsy put her head out of the door, but this was too much for the youth. His feelings were altogether beyond him; the sight of the adored one overcame him, and he turned on his heel and walked briskly away. We are told that in the fourth highest heaven of the Buddhists a touch of the hand satisfies love, in the fifth lovers simply gaze upon each other, and in the sixth existence in the same place is enough. Here was an example of it.

At nights there was sometimes a terrific noise from the guns, and though she might well have been inured to it by this time, Gipsy often lay awake listening, trying to distinguish between the Belgian or French guns which were behind and the German shells which came from the front. The Belgian batteries were so well concealed that even she and Mairi did not know where they were, though they could occasionally hear the "*ping*" of the telephone by which the results were communicated, possibly by their friend Captain de Wilde, who was observation officer. The departing shells had a sort of finished swish about them that sounded as if they said, "Now I'm off," and with a rush and report that shook the building they went; but those that arrived made a kind of despairing burst that shouted, "I've done my worst, and I've not killed you."

So long as no military orders to evacuate the *poste* were given, the Two stuck to it, however bad the bombardment, but they knew the summons might come at any moment. One night, when hopeless wakefulness possessed her, Gipsy lit the lamp, and saw that even the imperturbable Woffington was awake, chewing a piece of straw between his teeth, though Mairi slept soundly through the vibrating, ear-splitting crashes. In the intervals between these Mrs. Knocker said, "We may have to go, Woffy."

He nodded.

"Supposing the order came, and I said I wouldn't go, what would you do? Leave me?"

He considered the situation.

"I'd get a hold of you by the shoulder and give you a good un, and say, 'Ere, Knocker, up and 'op it!'" he decided at last.

At that second came the most appalling bang; the very house danced, for the lamp was shaken out! And Mairi, sitting up in the darkness amid her straw, cried out, "What is it? What has happened ?"

Though often there was comparatively little shelling in the day-time, it was impossible to make up a lost night's rest then, for people were in and out all day; if it wasn't the wounded needing attention, it was members of the ambulance corps flying out in their cars, perhaps bringing sightseers as to a show. Among the people who visited Pervyse from time to time were Ramsay Macdonald, Madame Curie, and Maxine Elliott, a grotesquely incongruous trio, within which every variety of nature and occupation incidental to civilized human nature might be fitted!

The *poste* was unique; such a thing had not only never been heard of, but never been thought of, before. There was even a certain amount of jealousy about it; others doing various kinds of work in Belgium pictured themselves in similar surroundings, but they never saw the gruesome side of the work there, the aching back and splitting head, and the constant anxiety. They only saw a singularly dramatic situation like the scene on a stage, with a singularly beautiful and inspiring couple of women in it, and it was not in human nature that they should not contemplate the possibility of making a similar setting for them-selves. What Gipsy thought of all this, especially of the reporters who hunted her out, may be gathered from the following private letter to a near relative:

"You tell me in your letters that you often see our names mentioned in the papers. I hope mine is not often there. I'm afraid I have fallen out with many reporters, but I hate all this penny-a-line business. I realize now that many decorations are not worth anything, and

113

one sees, on the other hand, so many really fine things done without a word of recognition, because they are done so quietly that they never get into the papers. I have a Belgian friend, a Dr. Van der Ghinst, who has probably never been heard of in England, and certainly does not wish to be—a quiet, splendid character. He was in Dixmude seven days and seven nights, absolutely alone, just keeping together the wounded men and civilians, and getting them out gradually from that veritable hell."

But if the visitors ignored the dangers in connection with that attractive setting, they were well known to the military. For some time Dr. Van der Ghinst had been uneasy as the German guns grew fiercer, and one day the good priest, who rode about on a fat white mare as round in the barrel as the variety on which the statues of our Stuart Kings are usually set, added his voice to the doctor's, telling the ladies that a terrible bombardment was expected, and they had better leave for safer quarters while there was time.

That same night, when everyone had gone, after—as the *poste* said—inconsiderately stirring up their feelings, Gipsy began to wonder if, after all, they ought not to go also; at any rate, the responsibility lay with her. Mairi would do whatever she was told, for among her great charms was one not usually associated with so young a girl—a loyal obedience to anyone whom she trusted. They began to discuss the question together, and finally, both being rather worked up, they decided to go down the village to the *génie* house, as they called it, and ask the advice of the Engineers.

It was a wild night, and the wind caught the rain and slung it this way and that, until it became as sharp as hail. Also it was very dark, so, clutching each other's hands and groping with their feet, the Two crept step by step along the ruined street, followed by the faithful Woffington.

They found the Engineer officers at supper, and were cordially welcomed. It was, indeed, an unexpected picture when Mrs. Knocker, with her brilliant eyes shining, peered in at the door, and Mairi peeped past her, with her fair hair uncovered, as she dashed the wet from her helmet cap.

The officers promptly suggested that they should pass the night there, as, being at the far end of the village from the front, the *génie* house was less likely to be shelled than the cellar. One of the younger men, whom they had nicknamed "Lieutenant Shrapnel," gallantly vacated his room, and so the Two slept there, with Woffington on a stretcher at their feet.

At five o'clock next morning a hideous alarum-clock went off with a scurry and shriek, and there was almost immediately cheery laughter and much scraping of feet, and some snatches of song that for the moment bewildered the two guests, who had forgotten where they were. At 6.30 came breakfast, consisting of toast, cream-cheese, fresh butter, and strawberry jam! In the middle of it an orderly arrived with orders for the officers to evacuate and go to Ypres. The Major waved the letter above his head. "*Dieu vous a bénit!*" he exclaimed, pointing out that Providence had evidently designed this order for the express purpose of allowing the poste to take up its quarters in this house instead of their own. This seemed to be the general opinion, and against fate there is no fighting. So when the last officer clattered off, Mairi, with a deep sigh of satisfaction, set to work and scrubbed and cleaned and wiped and dusted, and made the place a little more presentable.

After all, the officers came back, but not the meanest man among them would have disturbed the ladies; so they fixed themselves up in another half-ruined house elsewhere.

CHAPTER 11

The End of 1914

The piano in the new house proved better than the old one. There was also room for a double bed, a food cupboard, and other luxuries; after the cellar it seemed Paradise. At nights, wooden shutters had to be put up to hide the light, as the Two were now above ground. The glass in the windows had long been smashed. They had no idea yet of abandoning the cellar-house; they intended to keep that as a *poste*, for it was nearer to the trenches, but they themselves lived in the *génie* house. This, of course, entailed continual passing to and fro over the quarter of a mile or so that separated the two, and in the weeks that followed they grew used to ruined Pervyse in all its aspects. By the bright moonlight, with the black shadows lying in the corners, it suggested in a ghastly way a horribly decayed mouth with missing and broken teeth. By day it was very like one of the pit villages of the North, left to fall to pieces when the coal has run out, and abandoned by the whole population in a body; only in Pervyse there were more signs of violence than in such a melancholy village. Some of the houses were unrecognizable—just a heap of stones—and others had had a slice taken cleanly off the front, so that the whole interior lay revealed in naked intimacy. In some of these the furniture was still intact, and in others smashed and riddled with holes. In many cases, where it had been spared by the shells, it had been wantonly split up for firewood by the troops, and good polished mahogany and walnut lay in splinters.

It was the furniture that made the place so pitiful. In the colliery villages the inhabitants take their household goods with them when they remove, and there is no evidence of occupation cut suddenly short and left like an unhealed wound. To peep into one of the Pervyse houses, to see the pictures hanging all askew, the carpets or rugs

116

mouldy and stained, the china ornaments in atoms, the easy-chairs rotted and fallen, conveyed an awful sense of desolation. In one room, where the upper floor had been cut in two, a baby's cot balanced precariously by one of the rockers, and the coverlets were hanging down. Where was the baby occupant?

One day, as Gipsy passed along, she stopped, and started at hearing a sound of digging at the back of one of these houses. There was no shelling at the moment, and in the unusual stillness such a sound needed explanation. She passed round among the ruins, and came upon a very old woman, tall but bowed, with eyes like red pits, so inflamed were they with weeping. She was groping in the fallen *débris*, and had evidently found what she sought, for she stood up trying to hide beneath her shawl a cheap painted timepiece with a pent-house wooden roof and gaudy flowers smeared on the wood.

By one of those strange chinks in the general danger the clock-face had slipped through the bombardments and was unbroken. As the old woman gazed at it her weather-hardened face looked quite beautiful; she smiled at Gipsy, and without a word started to walk back again to Furnes, her *sabots* clanking on the cobbles. She had come out with one object, and had attained it. That clock had probably been a wedding gift, and was associated with the only days of pride and joy she had ever known. It was at least likely that she had lived out her span of life entirely in Pervyse, and never been elsewhere until torn up by the roots and flung out. For her there was nothing more to do but fade away; she could never take root again. Gipsy had nodded and smiled and tried to speak to her, but she found it impossible to make her understand, and as she stood there watching the bent figure hobble away, a sense of pity welled up in her so strongly that the tears came to her eyes. She shook them impatiently away. What use to drivel? There was work to be done. No wonder she writes: "I don't think I shall ever forget my life at Pervyse; it was all so strange at times, so pathetic, and yet there were moments when we giggled like children."

Continually terrible cases called for attention. Some of these were of men who had been sent out as scouts toward the German lines, and who had been seen and shot at. One night Alexandre, who slept in the kitchen of the *génie* house, came in saying that there was a wounded man somewhere down the road. Taking a lantern, Gipsy started out to find him; as usual, it was wet and very cold. She groped along, calling softly now and again, bracing herself for the sentry's challenge any moment. It came sharp and clear, "*Halte là!*" but when she explained the man knew her and let her go on.

Presently a faint groan drew her in the right direction. Wheeling toward it, she nearly went headlong into a huge shell-pit; then she discovered that the groans came from there. The man was at the bottom, lying in a foot of black water. She slipped and slithered down beside him, and found the poor fellow had an awful cut right across the head which had penetrated the skull. It was amazing that he lived, and still more so that he had managed to struggle so far as this in the direction of the *poste* before he fell into the pit. She bandaged him up first, and then, calling some passing soldiers for assistance, carried him into safety, and eventually he recovered sufficiently to go into Furnes.

Both women were much touched by the gratitude of the soldiers; however badly hurt, so long as they retained consciousness at all, they were never too far gone to try to express their thanks for what was done for them. And some of them were grievously hurt. One was shot in both shoulders by *mitrailleuse* bullets, and another had a bullet through the lung. A sergeant came in with a badly fractured leg and arm, and bullet wounds in his feet—"a terrible case, and just one of the pluckiest men I have ever seen. He smiled all the time, and was so brave and cheery—a fine soldier with a fine character." He died the next day.

The bravery of the men was indeed almost beyond belief. One day one of the soldiers appeared with a fearful wound. His right hand had been shot to bits while he was wearing a woollen glove. "I have never had such a disagreeable job as taking off that glove," Gipsy writes. "I could see every finger was blown to pieces, and the bits of glove mixed up everywhere, and the hand smashed; I expected every moment to pull off a finger with the glove. I cut as much as I could away, but it was all such a mess and muddle that I was afraid the scissors might do more harm than good." It must indeed have been a loathsome task, enough to try the nerves of the strongest.

One day, when some of the members of the corps came out in a car, seeing how white and worn Gipsy looked, one of them offered to stay for a night and let her have a rest, which she gladly accepted; but she had hardly made her preparations to go into the town, and had not got clear of the village, before a quite extraordinary number of wounded came in, and the lady sent after her begging her to come back, as it needed great experience to cope with such an influx.

A cheery crowd of naval officers turned up unexpectedly in a car from Dunkirk to see for themselves what the Two were doing. Among them was Mairi's friend the "Spaniard," as she, with her readiness at nicknames, had christened him. They were amazed at the sight of the village, and freely expressed their opinion that no ladies should be allowed to live there. They had seen many bad places since this war began, but this—you know—why, it was absurd, and they might be killed any time too! What were the authorities doing to allow it? Etc., etc., lot of old muddlers.

"The whole British Army objects to our being here," said Mairi; "but it can't do anything."

"Well, if I were one of the red-hats, I'd soon have you out of it! Why, you'd be safer on board. You might get killed—killed, you know, any time."

"Yes, we know all about that."

"But then it's ridiculous," the "Spaniard "protested feebly. "Really, Mairi, you'd much better marry me."

"So that you'd have power to keep me away, you think? Well, of course, if you are only proposing it on humanitarian grounds, I can tell you it wouldn't answer, because if ever I did such a mad thing, I'd come here just the same."

"You're doing a much madder one now," he said promptly.

"It's quite safe."

"Oh, rot! I say, how did the place get like this if there hasn't been shelling, and big shelling too?"

"Perhaps the Germans did it when they were here."

"Do you mean to tell me that shells don't drop in here now and again ?"

"Perhaps they do. What are they like? Describe one."

He looked at her, but she met him with the perfectly candid expression of a simple desire for information.

"Well, I'm—" he began, and then there was a long hiss and a scream and a crash, so near that they both instinctively leaped for the shelter of the *génie* house.

"That's punctured a hole in your terminological inexactitude," he said reproachfully. But before he finished speaking another came, and another, They were in for a bad bout. They continued to scream and crash, and presently the Belgian batteries near took up the antiphon and there was a real hullabaloo. This upset the naval men altogether. They absolutely buzzed in their anxiety.

"Do you mean to say you get this often? It's shameful! Someone ought to *make* you come away."

119

"Write to *The Times* about it," suggested Gipsy pleasantly. "And, meantime, don't you think we might have luncheon?"

"Luncheon? Oh, we brought a few things for you. We knew you couldn't buy much up here."

They hastened out, and unpacked from the car a royal supply, which, with the invariable consideration of men of the sea, they had carried up with them. They lunched royally off excellent ham, and tinned fruit, and other luxuries, but all the while the officers grumbled: they seemed to feel a personal enmity against the military who permitted such things. And finally they insisted on leaving behind one of the two cars in which they had come. "Then you can make tracks, if ever the time comes when you must," one of them said. This certainly was considerate, because frequently the car they used was away, taking wounded to Furnes, and in case of a sudden evacuation the Two would have been stranded.

"Dear fellows," said Gipsy, watching them bump off down the road in the other car.

"Very young," said Mairi, with an old-world air—"such boys!" As for her familiarity with shells, which Mairi had so innocently repudiated, this was the kind of thing that constantly happened: she was walking between the *génie* and the cellar-house, when she heard the shrill warning whistle, and sprang to one side, though really the broken ruins afforded no protection; then, as she went on, a small shell burst about fifty yards on the right. She concluded it was silly as well as useless to mind, so very deliberately strolled on down the middle of the street with her hands in the pockets of her tunic. Just as she reached the *poste*, another burst in front, sending the mud spurting up in all directions.

Gipsy had been watching her.

"Why on earth didn't you run ?" she inquired rather breathlessly, for it is much worse to watch another person in danger than to be in it yourself.

"It's not dignified when you are in khaki," answered Mairi gravely.

In her journal she constantly records some such remark as this:

Very little doing, except a few shrapnel coming in.

Yet the time came when they had to take notice. They were all at the cellar-house, and had just decided it was too much trouble to go back down the village for lunch. So Mairi cut up some potatoes and put them on to fry, saying that would stave off the pangs of hunger till tea-time, and then, in an instant, with no sort of warning, a shell really did land almost on the top of the house. It struck it somewhere, though, mercifully for them, not square, and for the moment it seemed as if the whole building was coming bodily to the ground. Each, catching her breath, thought instantaneously, "Is this really the end ?"

Bricks and mortar flew, but when the noise subsided they found they were still alive and quite unhurt, though the explosion had carried away a corner of the house; one of the men in the cellar opposite had been wounded by a splinter which flew in, and the Daimler car, which stood in a ruined outhouse, had been peppered. They counted twenty-eight holes in the bonnet, besides other damage.

When they had attended to the wounded man, they went on to the *génie* house, naturally feeling a little shaken, in spite of their nerve, and there they found the two doctors from the British Field Hospital to which the ambulance had been attached. These men had heard the explosion and seen part of the cellar-house collapse, and were dreadfully upset at the idea of women being in such peril. They couldn't get used to it. One of the soldier servants standing by looked at them open-mouthed, and exclaimed:

"*Vous n'avez pas peur?*"

What could they reply but, "*Pas du tout*," though limbs were still trembling and hearts palpitating? He was a cheery soul, and encouraged them by remarking complacently, "*Les Boches bombard era encore cette maison-ci.*"

Reinforcements were being hurried up. The fighting at Nieuport was furious, and the whole line was being attacked with unusual vigour; all around there was stir and menace. What had preceded seemed almost peaceful in comparison; anything might happen these days. Coming out of the *génie* house in the afternoon Gipsy passed a couple of the great patient *mitrailleuse* dogs who had been struck by a splinter of shell; their shaggy paws were being bound up by the gunners. She went over to help, regardless of the risk and exposure, and had them brought into the kitchen, and one of them licked her hand with his rough tongue, for all the world as if he were trying to express gratitude like his masters.

Seeing that the bombardment continued to be pretty furious for days, it was natural that the naval men should turn up again to see how the Two were getting on; they seemed to think it a sort of personal slur that they should be under fire while they themselves were not. The "Spaniard "got no chance that night, for Mairi was surrounded. Her type appealed peculiarly to the men of the sea; they saw in her all that they adored in the vision of a "fresh British girl," and her cheery aloofness and lack of susceptibility heightened the flame. "You'll have to marry some time," one of them told her, with a touch of maliciousness in his tone. "No use meeting evils half-way," she retorted gaily.

In spite of their anxiety, the officers were full of hope and expectancy; everywhere it was said that the offensive would soon be begun, and that the Germans would be driven back. The *Taubes* certainly had an idea also that something was afoot, for their visits were persistent, and hardly a day passed that one or more did not soar above, to be tackled by the French airmen. One day the Two watched with intense eagerness a fight between aviators in which neither eventually got the better of the other, though the manoeuvres and dodges were splendid to watch. The Frenchman at last daringly dropped headlong on to his antagonist, endeavouring to smash one of his wings, missed by inches, as it appeared to the rapt onlookers, and fell too far to recover himself before his adversary flew away.

Another time, seeing a *Taube* overhead, they ran out to look at it, and heard the firing of a *mitrailleuse* somewhere near. They could not make out where the firing came from. It couldn't be from the Germans, who were too far off; it couldn't be from their own men, because the bullets were beginning to splash around. Nearer came the deadly splashes until they realized they must beat a quick retreat into shelter of some kind, and it was only then they grasped the fact that the *Taube* man was leaning over his machine deliberately potting them with a quick-firing gun!

At the very top of the village, near the railway line and the trenches, stood the church, with its high rectangular tower, which had for some time been used as an observation station by Captain de Wilde, and was now unsafe. It had parted company with the nave and leaned forward at an angle, and the military men decided it must come down. They sent a message to the *poste* inviting them to attend the ceremony, so they walked out along the stretch of melancholy street that they traversed so often in a day and were growing to hate. The first violent explosion under the church tower produced apparently no result at all. It was followed by another, but though the tower looked as if the push of a hand must send it over, it never stirred, and then there was a long interval, possibly five minutes, which seemed like fifteen to the spectators. "It's not going at all," said Mairi, as the third explosion rang out, but it was! Very slowly and with dignity the tower seemed to turn on its axis, revealing a gaping wound all down its side, and then it subsided almost gently. It was a melancholy sight, as if some living thing had received the *coup de grâce*. The huge clock-face, rescued from the *débris*, was sent down as a present to the *poste*; they found they couldn't take this rather unwieldy souvenir inside, so propped it up against the wall.

It was a sad day when the 9th Regiment, which had been at Pervyse from the first, had orders to move elsewhere, saddest of all because their good friend Dr. Van der Ghinst had to go too. Pervyse was the most coveted position in the whole Belgian line by this time; every man in the army had heard the story of the wonderful ladies who were there to tend and sympathize. The incoming regiment proved itself quite as appreciative and grateful as the last, but one day the Two were amused to receive a note from the 9th, saying that if the *poste* wasn't happy at Pervyse with their successors, they had better come along and join them in their new quarters!

It had been decided that Gipsy must be spared at Christmas to pay a brief visit home to see her little boy Kenneth, and in the meantime others must carry on the work as best they could. As she was the moving spirit and originator of the whole scheme, and she alone had made it feasible by her personality and capability, it was like losing the soul when she went. But Mairi by this time was a skilled assistant, and far beyond the average girl of her age in steadiness and sense. She was the first to see that her friend's highly strung nature was worn by the incessant noise and calls upon her sympathy, and by the burden of wearing responsibility, and must have relaxation. For though indomitable in spirit, Gipsy was built in a delicate mould. The way was made easier because Lady Dorothie Feilding agreed to come to live with Mairi in Pervyse while Gipsy was away.

The farewells were touching, including letters of God-speed from the officers, loving good wishes and evidences of a wealth of devotion from the men which she warmly appreciated.

She ran into Furnes in a car, and while there went to see Miss Macnaughtan, who was then working at her soup kitchen. The station was lit only by a dim swinging lamp, and through it there defiled a procession of weird figures that might be the vision of a nightmare or a page from Dante's *Inferno*. Many of them came straight from the trenches wearing their torn and motley clothes, and they were band-

MERRY MEN FROM THE TRENCHES

THE TOTTERING CHURCH TOWER

FLOODS

WHERE SOME OF THE FALLEN WERE BURIED.

aged so that their outlines were distorted or their faces were invisible, while many lacked limbs. The humped-up look of the stretcher cases added a depressing touch of its own. And there was a curious silence pervading the waiting train. Gipsy walked down beside it, saying a quiet word of encouragement here and there, and suddenly from among the disguised crowd one stepped out, and grasping her hand in his left, the only one available, poured out on her a stammering tale of recognition, reminding her she had tended him at Dixmude. Since then he had been back again to the front, and a second time been wounded. By the light of this it seemed more miraculous than ever that she, who had been under continual firing, should have escaped. Among the men was one German, white and terrified, expecting nothing less than torture or death; wild-eyed, he refused even a cigarette, lest it should be poisoned!

The weather was bitterly cold; mud and rain all the way—a horrid crossing.

What a contrast to be awakened on Christmas morning by the glad cries of her little son, who had discovered the joys of his full stocking! She could hardly realize where she was. The softness of the yielding bed, the white sheets, the perfect stillness and comfort and cleanliness of everything, seemed to sink into her very bones. How little people who took these things as a matter of course every day of their lives knew of the hell out there!

Meantime, Mairi was helped by Lady Dorothie Feilding, who was fully seasoned to danger by many a ghastly experience. These two girls, for there were not very many years between them, carried on the work successfully. In one of her private letters home Gipsy says of Mairi:

She has never shirked a day or night; always cheerful and bright, and absolutely to be depended on.

In spite of all her wisdom, she was youthful enough to feel the glamour of Christmas. "Only one Christmas card and a bunch of mistletoe," she remarks.

She began her day by the good "tidy-up" which her soul loved, and after having washed up the dishes, she and her companion began to give out some socks which had been sent for the soldiers, when "Crash came a shell! *Crash! Crash! Crash!* Nothing but falling bricks and the whistle of arriving shells for half an hour. One hit the house opposite us, brought all the tiles down; two hit our house and came through the wall; shrapnel burst just at our door, hitting the soldiers sheltering in our passage. The clock-dial standing against the door was riddled with holes, and all the smoke and smell of powder blew in at the door! A nice Christmas present to send us!"

She attended to the slightly wounded men, talked to the old priest who had turned up to beg a shirt for himself, and then, helped by the Lady Dorothie, hung up little flags to make the room gay for the Christmas dinner. Even the candle had a paper lantern round it.

The dinner itself was a triumph. Ox-tail soup, cold fowl, fried potatoes, plum pudding, mince pies, sweets, chocolate biscuits, nuts, and even crackers! The guests at this feast were Dr. Munro, Captain Robert de Wilde, and another man, and one of them supplied champagne.

A raging gale the next day blew down everything that hung tottering in Pervyse; the floods rose, streams of water came through the roof of the *génie* house where the shrapnel had burst it, and in the midst of all this Mairi received distinguished callers—the colonel of the *Chasseurs* and General Melis, Chief of the Belgian Army Medical Service. The fame of the *poste* was growing!

On the last day of 1914 Gipsy returned.

CHAPTER 12

Waiting for Attack

After having seen death around in so many guises, it seems natural for Mairi Chisholm to open her New Year's diary with the terse and unaffected words:

"What will 1915 bring to us? Death, I suppose, to many—I wonder which ones!" Fortunately they were both spared; not a scratch did they get, though they worked the whole year through in the thick of the danger.

For women, especially women unaccustomed to continuous physical exertion, the difficulty is to keep on doing the same thing, as many heads of canteens have found. A woman in her own home may do a little housework, but there is nothing to prevent her knocking off and resting when she feels it too much; to "keep on keeping on," as Mr. J. C. Snaith has it, is the test. There are hundreds of women willing to do a day a week in canteens, handing out food to munition workers or soldiers, but even the one continuous day, always the same day, seems more than many are able to manage, and it is the units among the tens who hold on regularly. But to go on as the Two did, day in, day out, while months ran into years, with every nerve on the alert, under a strain both physical and mental, is a wonderful feat.

The New Year made them both very busy, as the fighting continued active, and the urgency of the work compelled Gipsy to break off her journal, which does not begin again until September; but sturdy Mairi continued hers, and Gipsy's letters home fill the gap.

In the very beginning of the year, she took over a party of six soldiers to England; they were going to convalesce in a little house which had been given by friends. That journey was a night-mare. The men were very ill—they were not merely slight cases; three of them were on stretchers. The crossing was rough as it could be; all the half-dozen were sea-sick, and, as some of the poor fellows were stomach cases, and ought never to have had this added strain, their condition became pitiable. Each separate one needed a nurse to himself, and in the close quarters, with the violent motion of the ship, Gipsy had to do everything for them all, with only the help of anyone who might happen to be there. The responsibility for those poor racked bodies was hers. When they drew near Dover, it was so rough no pilot would come out, and they tossed about three weary hours outside, until by desperate signalling as to the condition of the wounded on board a pilot was obtained. They got into Dover at nine at night instead of five o'clock, as expected, and the additional hours of tossing about seemed spun out into eternity for each suffering man. The last train up to town had gone, and as arrangements had been made on the supposition that they would be in London that night, there was no accommodation ready at the town.

Mr. G———, one of the ambulance corps, had fortunately come to meet the boat, and had got some ambulances. From the pier Gipsy telephoned to the military hospital to ask that her patients might be taken in, but there was no room. Then she tried the King's Head Hotel, and was able to get them in there. Naturally they were all frightfully ill with pain and exhaustion, and all night long she had to run from one to the other, helped by an R.A.M.C. officer who fortunately happened to be staying there. She must have been feeling very bad herself, but she never mentions this in her account of the incident; all she says is, "They were splendid."

This was on a Saturday. The men were taken up by train to London next day and across to Euston, and here, owing to the scarcity of Sunday trains, it was impossible to avoid a delay of five hours. Out of the six sufferers, four were really in a very precarious state and one in particular very nearly died. It was an immense relief when at last they reached their goal and were handed over to the willing helpers waiting for them. But the experience was enough to turn anyone's hair grey, and it is easily understood that Gipsy found it actually "restful" to get back to Pervyse. She was knocked up by the experience, and looked forward to a decent night's rest, but instead of that the guns split the air all night long.

The floods at this time were terrible; it looked almost as if Pervyse itself might be inundated. The ground was saturated, and the water rose a foot high in the cellar, so that it could not be used at all. In the *génie* house they were dry underfoot, but in spite of all they could do

"Nothing Doing."

The injured horses.

MRS. KNOCKER AND MISS CHISHOLM.

to stop it the rain dripped through the cracked and battered roof into the living-room. The Two lived in oil-skins and rubber boots as they paddled to and fro on necessary errands. The men in the trenches were knee-deep in water, and agonizing cases of cramp, rheumatism, and neuritis, came in daily. To add to all these joys, the Two discovered a new form of danger which had so far escaped their notice; this was the risk from their own shrapnel when the empty cases fell in the village.

"We were watching some aeroplanes when we heard a most quaint sound—an indistinct low whistle, like a shell, and yet different from any kind of shell we had met. We heard it for some time, and were puzzled by it, but came to the conclusion it certainly was getting nearer, and quite suddenly, with one impulse, we both fled like rabbits into our hole, and an empty shrapnel case pitched on the side of the road exactly where we had been. It was from our own shrapnel. We had never thought of that."

A brief record of some of the cases dealt with from day to day is given by Mairi. A sergeant was brought in on a stretcher, but he was already dead, half his head having been blown off. Another man had gone out of his mind with the noise and horror; another had his hand badly scalded; several had severe internal pains brought on by inflammation in the cold, and one morning at 3.30 they were woke up to tend a man in supreme agony who had had the bad luck to blow off his own hand with his rifle. He had somehow managed to shoot off his right thumb, and the same bullet had gone on and penetrated his left arm. How he had done it remained for ever a conundrum—there seemed to be no sort of attitude that even a contortionist could take to manufacture that particular damage.

All this time the Two had paid for their own food, and had never asked a penny from the Belgians. They lived precariously on whatever they happened to get. "We had a ham to boil, and I made the bread-crumbs," said Mairi, showing that they did not neglect any amenities within their reach. Another day "An officer shot eight sparrows, which he gave us, and I started in and plucked the little jossers. Quite a job !"

The occasional runs into Furnes to fetch stores were a pleasant break in lives which, though full of incident, tended to become monotonous. In Pervyse they had to spend most of their days in "two dingy, smelly, little *postes*" the only alternative being that depressing street with its brooding death. The rattling drive into the town was over roads pock-marked with shell-holes, varied by an occasional bump when the car ran off the *pavé* and landed in the mud. On these occasions they had to get out and heave her back; once they had even to use a jack, and, as shells were flying about and they were well within the radius, it required some nerve. When they arrived in Furnes, "we had a mad rush round the shops and grabbed all the stores we could find; it all seemed so new and interesting after a desolate village. Then a mad rush back again over the same old bumpy, holey road, and home to our tumbled-down cottage. Yet you have no idea what a great treat it all seems to us."

The first time they did this in January, though they were only away two hours, they found that it was just that scrap of time in which the Queen of the Belgians had chosen to pay them a visit. They could have wept with disappointment at having missed her. "We were as sick as death," says Mairi in her expressive slang, "and it will take us some time to get over it."

There were other visitors of much less consequence who had found them at home, and that she, the heroine Queen who had been the inspiration of Belgium in these its darkest days, should have missed them caused them acute chagrin. The Mayor of Paris was among their visitors one day, and Gipsy remarks ironically:

> There never is a wounded man here when these great folks arrive. I think I shall have to get a tame *blessé* and keep him permanently bandaged on a stretcher on the floor, and when I see them coming get busy and look interesting with hot chocolate and bandages.

They had grown to be quite expert in the matter of judging the different kinds of shells, and even their size, from the noise they made, and by now they were accustomed to the crash of the naval guns from the coast, which pitched huge shells right over Pervyse. One day, when the bombardment was very bad, a priest and some soldiers ran into the *génie* house to recover their breath and shelter before going on. The shells from the German lines seemed to be dropping all round that particular spot. "They must be passing over the cellar-house, anyhow," Gipsy remarked; "they can't be in two places at once."

But they could, and were, for some of them at any rate fell close by one *poste*, and some near the other, exactly as if those two houses had been the only objectives. The cellar-house itself was not hit, but it escaped by a miracle, for, judging from the destruction around, at least a hundred shells must have pitched close by it, and the first line of trenches just behind was churned up into mud. Luckily there did not happen to be any soldiers there on that particular day, and the damage done was trifling. The total bag was the priest slightly, and one soldier badly, wounded, for all that expenditure of shell-power. But it was obvious that the cellar-house was untenable, and sadly they decided to give it up altogether. The shelling now came very close to it constantly, and what with the wet and the danger, it seemed foolish to try to hold on to it, especially now that they had got the other *poste* where the necessary work could be carried on. .

One morning they agreed to go together to the cellar-house to bring up the few things that remained there. At the moment there was, as Mairi phrases it, "nothing doing," and they walked along light-heartedly. Close by the cellar-house half a dozen of the soldiers' horses were stabled in a dilapidated outhouse, and Gipsy, who was a good horsewoman and passionately fond of horses, went in to pet them. She and Mairi stood there a minute or two stroking the soft noses of their friends and feeding them with bits, and then went on. It did not take ten minutes to pick up what they wanted in the cellar, and they had just started homewards when "out of the blue" there came a most appalling explosion and then the smashing and falling of bricks. The noise was quite different from that of a shell bursting on the roadway, and they knew that something had happened. Wheeling round, they saw clouds of mortar and smoke and dust rolling about, and found that the room above the cellar was smashed to pieces, the last remnants had gone.

Worse still, the stable had suffered too, and regardless of the fact that usually three shells pitch in quick succession about the same place, they ran back to see what had occurred. The cellar-house had only caught a little of the explosion, but it was obvious a large shell must have plumped right into the stable, for three of the horses lay dead, and the other three, badly hurt, struggled feebly. It was an agonizing sight, like a slaughter-house, with the crazy walls and damp straw splashed red with blood. It was, perhaps, more like "War," as seen in the imagination, than anything they had yet come across. One of the soldiers came to take the three surviving horses to L'Espérance, and led them up the village. When Gipsy saw the miserable procession, she realized at once that the poor animals were too severely injured to walk all that way, so she stopped them at the *poste* and had them put in the garage shed.

All that day she spent in alternately trying to do what she could and "annoying every officer I saw, from a General to a Lieutenant," to send a vet. At length, at nine that evening, a vet came. He shot two of the remaining horses, saying their case was hopeless, while the Two stood beside him holding the lantern, with the wind and rain moaning round, and the only survivor looking on with patient eyes, as if he understood all about it. But alas, he had to go too! The vet took immense pains, and dug bits of shell out of him all over, but his case was hopeless, and the next day he shared the fate of his fellows. Both girls felt this deeply. Animals had a tremendous hold on their hearts, and it seemed a pitiable *finale* to the little cellar-house, now finally abandoned.

From henceforth a new chapter of the story was opened, and they lived in the *génie* house altogether and tended the men there. A notice was put up outside the cellar-house directing all who needed aid to come on farther. The *genie* was in reality not so safe as the cellar-house had been, because it was entirely above ground, but it was a little further from the guns, and one terror that had haunted both of the friends, though they had never confessed it in words, was laid to rest. At least, whatever happened, they would be always together. It had been secret agony to think that, with the coming and going from one *poste* to the other, one might be caught and smashed while the other was not there. More than ever they determined to cling to each other, always and everywhere, so that in death they should not be divided.

In the midst of all this a painter came to paint their portraits. And in the words of the irrepressible Mairi, "We had to stand at fearful angles for unknown times." Tension was still growing, in spite of these frivolous incidents. Before the end of the month Furnes, having been heavily bombarded, was evacuated by the British hospital, which had so far "stuck it out," and though their connection with the hospital, or indeed any practical association with the ambulance corps, had long ceased, this cutting of the thread made them feel more than ever that they stood alone in their little shell-swept village.

Custom breeds contempt, and so many times had they heard that the Germans might make a big attack and break through that they had grown to smile inquiringly at such rumours and pass on, forgetting all about it in five minutes. But now the rumour grew and gathered force, and was backed up by authorities there was no gainsaying; yet, as no orders had come through from headquarters about evacuating their post, they stayed where they were. On the evening of January 25 some of the officers whom they had not seen for a little while came in, and seemed surprised to find them still there. They obviously did not want to be alarming, and yet their grave looks and general air of tension indicated that something unusual was expected.

The girls questioned them, and made them admit that they had every reason to expect a terrific onslaught before the morning. However, it was too late now to take any steps toward evacuation, even had they wished to; there was nothing for it but to see it out. It was the waiting in inaction that was most trying. Again and again both of them say in their journals, "I don't mind the shells while I am busy with the wounded; I forget all about them." But to sit and wait for this unknown terror, that was indeed a strain on nerve power. For the time all was quiet—an uncanny stillness that was saturated with suspense!

The officers continued to come in and out, going away to see to this or that item of supply, and returning again graver than before.

Man after man got up and went out to hold mysterious whispered colloquies in the passage with despatch-riders; the atmosphere grew more tense with portent. Visions of the grey-clad Germans, lust-mad, bestial, pouring in like a herd of wild beasts, haunted the women.

The room in which they sat has been described by Mary Rinehart, an American writer, who visited them here. "What a strange room it was, furnished with odds and ends from the shattered houses about! A bed in the corner, a mattress-bed on the floor, a piano in front of the shell-holed windows—a piano so badly cracked by shrapnel that panels of the woodwork were missing and keys gone—two or three odd chairs, and what had once been a book-case, and in the centre a pine table laid for a meal. Every opening of the door into the corridor brought a gale of wind through the ruined house—hardly a foot of the plaster interior of that room was whole. The ceiling was riddled, so were the walls; in the centre of the former was a great bulge."

One of the other ladies happened by an unlucky incident to be at the *poste* that night; it was the American, whose *forte* was piano-playing. Presently she sat down and began to play on the hacked and battered piano, that had once been used only for hymn-tunes strummed out on Sunday evenings by a respectable bourgeois family. The melody that was its soul now found utterance and streamed out from her finger-tips, and floating away through the chinks in the rough improvised shutters, carried the souls of her hearers up into the world of great spaces lit by stars. Even the men who brought those fateful messages paused for a moment at the shot-battered entrance outside as the music drifted round them.

On and on she played, until one o'clock came, and still no guns were heard. One by one the officers slipped away, all except one who was on picket duty. As Mrs. G—— paused, letting the notes die away, a far-distant sound of *mitrailleuses* came over from the trenches. All the party were now very white, and it was long since anyone had uttered a word.

Soon after a quick step was heard on the road, and there was a little stir of expectancy while Corporal Delmotte of the *Mitrailleurs* came in. They had not seen him for a day or two, as he had been on leave. He saluted the captain, explaining that all the reserve *mitrailleuse* men on leave had been called back and centred in Pervyse, as a big attack was expected at earliest dawn. Even now, he suggested, there was time for the ladies to go back to Furnes. His proposal was no sooner understood than dismissed: they had had no orders—unanswerable reply. But to back it up, woman-like, they added: what better would they be if they did go? Supposing that accursed host burst through, would they be any better in deserted Furnes than here?

"So we passed this strange, strange night." But the strangest incident of all was to come. Mrs. G—— had flung herself face downward on one of the beds and fallen asleep. Gipsy and Mairi linked arms and stole quietly to the door, with the captain and corporal behind. They felt the street as vibrant as an electric wire, though all the sounds were muffled and any orders were in whispers. They had stood there only two minutes, when behind them on the side remote from the German lines they saw an electric torch flash out—once, twice, dot, dash, dot, stop! It was away out in the fields, and even though they could not read the message, there could be no doubt of its purport: it was telling the Germans what reinforcements were being brought up. A bright blue light from the German side sprang out in reply.

The man beside them gave a deep hiss in his throat, "*S-s-sacré!*" There was a hurried whisper, then a quick scuffle and rush as the corporal with a detachment of three swept past to nail the traitor in his lair. They did not get him, needless to say—traitors are far too wily to remain where bayonets may pin them to the door-post.

By five o'clock the two friends had fallen peacefully asleep, utterly unable to keep their eyes open any longer, and when they reopened them in broad daylight everything was as usual, and the Germans had not materialized, but all day long came in an avalanche of wounded, which showed what the cost of holding them up had been!

CHAPTER 13

Shelled Out

General Jacquez, commanding the Belgian Army, had been once or twice to call upon the ladies of the *poste*. But when he came in a day or two after this, accompanied by three staff officers, there was something official in his air which set them on the alert. Mrs. Knocker and Mairi stood before him, a little confused at the magnificence of his salute, which had a sort of special impressiveness about it. They watched him, wondering what on earth was coming as he drew out a paper; was this at last a "notice to quit"? The general's air of satisfaction hardly portended that.

He said with great dignity, "I have been sent by His Majesty the King of the Belgians to inform you that he has created you Knights (*Chevaliers*) of the Order of Leopold II., and I ask you, ladies, to accept my most sincere congratulations," and he handed them the King's Order.

For a moment they stood stock-still, dumbfounded, not realizing all it meant, only perceiving with a rush of gladness that what they had *tried* to do had been known and appreciated by the hero-King, for whom they cherished the deepest admiration.

It was so unexpected that it was a little difficult to assimilate. From time to time some of the officers had let fall hints of a possible decoration, but that it would be other than a medal, bestowed at the end of the war, had never entered their heads. It was not until General Jacquez had left that they were able to think coherently, and then they drank each other's health in a glass of Horlick's malted milk.

It came out later that the king's attention had been drawn to them since that first awful day at Melle, when they had insisted on going back under fire and bringing out the German wounded. The episode of their driving to Furnes, alone and unprotected, five German prisoners, had also been brought to the king's notice; Mrs. Knocker's marvellously heroic work in driving the ambulances under terrible conditions, when even hardened chauffeurs gave way, had made her name famous; and their steady and purposeful work under constant fire at Pervyse, where the king had himself seen them, had been the culminating point.

One thing had led to another, and had it not been for the previous work, which had shown such unusual qualities of pluck and devotion, the development of this *poste* at Pervyse could never have been permitted. It was only very exceptional women who could be trusted to keep their heads amid such strange and trying conditions, which demanded the utmost discretion and resource. And now that the King had set his seal upon the work and given it his countenance they were in quite a different position. Gipsy recognized with joy, not only the personal honour, which she valued as highly as anyone could, but the greatly increased opportunities of usefulness it opened the way for in the future.

The sequel came in a message from the king, asking whether they would like him to send the insignia, or whether they would go to him to receive the decoration at his hands. They chose the latter, naturally. The day fixed was February 1, on which many of the officers were to be decorated; curiously enough, it coincided with the birthday of little Kenneth, Mrs. Knocker's only child. The two who were to be decorated had agonisedly inquired of everyone exactly what was the etiquette of the occasion, and what they ought to say and do; but they were both extremely nervous, and a cold, blustery day did not improve matters. Here is Mairi's description of that nerve-trying morning:

A lot of dashing round trying to find things, and vainly hoping to improve our appearances; falling over everything, and getting in each other's way.

The wind blew straight from the sea, bringing with it a tang that bit pink cheeks and made noses unbecomingly red. They were clad in weather-stained khaki knickers, long leather coats, and high boots, with khaki wool caps bearing in brass letters the number of the army division to which they were attached. They stood ranged in rank at the end of a long line of officers for about three hours. Mairi is much the fairer of the two, and her clear blue eyes have something in them of the glint seen in the eyes of a man who knows not fear. They are so limpid and candid, no one could dream of the horrid experiences and revolting sights which have bitten deep into the life of this brave little Scot, and have, so she says, made her feel ten years older since she went to Belgium. Mrs. Knocker's eyes are hazel, or, as someone has called them, "khaki-colour"!

All the hastily acquired ideas concerning etiquette fled from their minds when the immensely tall king towered above them, his sad, deep-blue eyes looking down upon them as he pinned the Cross on their tunics. He talked with them a long time in English, and asked many questions about Pervyse, expressing his personal gratitude for their work among his beloved soldiers; and when he had passed on to decorate others, they realized with something like dismay that he had so completely enthralled them they had quite forgotten to curtsey, and had talked with him as if he had been a kind friend or one of the officers who came familiarly in and out of the *génie* house.

The tufty grass was iced, and when they came to themselves again they found their feet were too!

Miss May Sinclair, in an article in the *Daily Chronicle* about this time, says:

> The special correspondent has missed Mrs. Knocker altogether, and yet perhaps it is by her services and those of Miss Mairi Chisholm that the Munro Ambulance has best proved the fitness of women in the actual field.

She goes on to speak of what they had endured.

> The net of death around a field ambulance is at times woven so fine that only by a miracle can they escape it.
> There was no limelight on the field at Melle, on that road between Dixmude and Furnes, or among the blood and straw in the cellar at Pervyse.

In a private letter to one of Mrs. Knocker's near relations Miss Sinclair says:

> You will have heard of the great honour that has just been bestowed on her (Mrs. Knocker) and Miss Chisholm: they have both been made *Chevaliers de l'Ordre de Leopold II.*, which is a great honour, and given by the King himself. I dare say she has not been able to tell you how thoroughly she has deserved it; but you will realize that. I am rejoiced that it has come so soon, and come to them alone of the corps, for there is not one of them that has done such fine work so unobtrusively and untir-

ingly or shown quite such splendid courage as they. And it has been so sad to know all this, and to see other people getting the credit for what they have done the establishing and carrying through of the dressing-station at Pervyse was done by Mrs. Knocker and Miss Chisholm only. I hear that there are several conjectures as to what particular deed has won them this honour. . . .

I wish I could have done more to make their splendid work known as it should be. It was enough honour for any woman to have been with them and to have seen some of it.

However, when the new decorations were freshly pinned on their tunics they were very shy about them, and, buttoning their leather coats over them, they went into the town to try to buy something "special" to take back to celebrate the occasion, and to their great joy managed to procure a leg of mutton! In the inn they encountered some of the naval officers who had not been present at the ceremony, and were surprised to see them both together so far from their "cheery little village." Their curiosity was uncompromisingly snubbed, but men of the sea are not easily put off when they want to know anything, and at last they wormed out the secret. Then they called, "Three cheers for King Albert," until the roof rang.

"It was Justice with a big 'J' when you were singled out," said one of them cordially. "So far as I know, you are actually the only women right up in the firing-line at all—and you jolly well shouldn't be," he added, after a pause.

It was true. Nurses work at base hospitals which are established beyond the fire-zone; some canteens are fairly near, but none can be said to be right up at the front. But these two girls had not only been there, but been there all the time, which is more than could be said of the soldiers themselves, who were withdrawn and changed at intervals. Members of the ambulance corps had dashed in and out and given a hand now and again, but Gipsy and Mairi were the only two who had, in the slangy but expressive phrase, "stuck it out" all the time. The *poste* was due to them, and them alone. It was Gipsy's idea, and her personality only had made it possible. Yet this view was not taken in all quarters; there were some who loved the limelight, and having been in it pretty frequently, thought the king must have suffered from myopia to pass them over, though as a matter of fact he had really proved his uncommon keenness of vision.

141

On their arrival back at Pervyse the Two found themselves plunged into a white heat of excitement; the *avant-poste*, right out on the long road across the water, had been taken by the Germans! So often had they visited that *poste* at nights with jugs of hot chocolate that they felt a keen personal interest in it, and when the Belgian guns began to talk and express their views of the matter they listened with eager attention, wondering anxiously if the shells fell straight and true. The noise, of course, was terrific; this was no time for economising munitions, and the many batteries went to work whole-heartedly to help out the infantry, and by ten o'clock that evening the *poste* was recovered.

Now that the king had recognized their work it was on a different footing altogether. The Headquarter Staff approached Gipsy with a request that she would open another *poste*, similar to that at Pervyse, elsewhere on the front. A higher compliment could hardly have been paid to the utility of the work, but there were great difficulties in the way of compliance. It would be impossible to have the two *postes* sufficiently near together to be run at once; even the coming and going between the two houses in little Pervyse had been a greater strain than they had anticipated, and yet, if the *postes* were to be run separately, who was to look after them? Excellently trustworthy as Mairi had proved herself, she was too young to be left in charge of one alone. So they asked for time to consider the matter, and meantime went to Wimereux for a few days' holiday with friends, and while there celebrated Mairi's nineteenth birthday. She had a birthday-cake with a Cupid and candles in the centre, though the Cupid surely must have been a jest, as he was not in Mairi's line at all!

When they returned on March 3 they were greeted by a salvo of shells, and the pluck and nerve possessed by nineteen-years-old can best be gauged by the following incident:

Two men were brought into the *poste* too far gone for anything to be done; they were bad head cases, the most shocking of all forms of wounds, and the brains were protruding. Mairi says:

> Immediately they were dead we took them out and put them in the back yard; shells were coming in all the time. We helped to search through the clothes of the poor fellows. One, a boy of nineteen, had only been in the trenches two days. As I was searching through the pockets of a big overcoat, I came across the brains of one of the men, evidently blown there by the force of the explosion—(and she adds sedately), a very curious

incident.

The shelling continued with unabated force, and the Belgian doctor, Martin, grew uneasy, saying the *poste* was no place for wounded men to be in, and they ought to get away at once. But what could be done? It was also much too dangerous to take them down that shell-swept street, so for the time they had to remain where they were. The next day terrible cases continued to accumulate, nearly all these ghastly head-wounds, which proved so fatal that one after another of the poor fellows had to be carried out and laid on the verandah. Poor lads, only about Mairi's own age, who had gone up singing to the trenches the evening before! All the morning of the 4th the cruel, heart-tearing work went on. Dr. Martin, who was one of the best and staunchest of men, slipped out to get his lunch with the officers, but returned directly afterwards.

He was wanted elsewhere, and had only come back to get his mackintosh; while he stood there a military ambulance came up to carry away the dead bodies. It had required some fortitude for the chauffeur to bring it through, for the shelling was still going on, though it was not quite so bad as it had been. The chauffeur leapt from the car, and with that desperate feeling which leads every-one to rush to shelter, even though they know it affords no real protection, he ran into the kitchen, where were another chauffeur and the orderlies. As he did so, there came an appalling crash, one of those which spoke of something more than a mere burst, and they all knew the house itself had been struck. Stones and mortar came clattering down, and stray bricks flew about amid a great cloud of evil-smelling smoke and choking dust. The chauffeurs and orderlies staggered through into the living-room, where the shock had been slighter, holding their arms up over their faces to protect their eyes, which nevertheless were smarting with bits and splinters.

As the confusion slowly calmed down, like a death-knell in the hearts of the two devoted women rang the word "Evacuation!" They knew there was no chance of staying after this. Once already they had hung on to a *poste* until it had actually been struck and they had been driven out, and now they must retreat a second time!

"Get on your hats and coats, and make a rush for it," someone shouted. The chauffeur, recovering himself, gallantly went first, expecting every second the impact of another large shell, and got his car turned ready for the rest; then they all rushed out, tumbling into it

143

pell-mell, knowing that each second's delay might cost them all their lives. So they fled, leaving a piece of their hearts behind at the dear little *poste* which had sheltered them. They were followed down the road by the Belgian doctor in his own car, but before they reached the *brasserie*, where was the headquarters of Colonel Flébus, the doctor was struck and fell. There was a boy from the Congo, personal attendant of one of the officers, a faithful lad who stuck to his master through thick and thin, and many times proved his brave heart. He dashed out and carried the doctor in triumphantly, and when he was examined they thought his wounds were not serious, and he would live for many a day to continue the work he had done so unweariedly. Alas, gangrene set in and he died!

The Two were welcomed at the *brasserie*, and the colonel said that of course they must give up all idea of being at the *poste* for the future. Once the German guns had been trained actually upon it, it was only a matter of time when it would be demolished altogether. So miserably they waited, their hearts heavy with sorrow, until about five o'clock, when, the shelling having subsided, they went back to collect all they could from the ruined house. It was a dismal sight. The kitchen was a shapeless mass, and in falling had made a natural tomb for the poor dead bodies on the verandah. The walls were riddled, and one soldier who had taken refuge in the shed adjoining, that they called the garage, had been killed as he stood.

It was very difficult for the two friends to know where to go now they were refugees. However, that evening found them at La Panne, a little place on the sea-coast, the most miserable-looking objects you could find, covered with mud and blood, and terribly depressed at this wholesale retreat forced upon them, which came across their high spirits like a shameful bruise.

They remained ten days or so at La Panne, walking along the sandhills and thinking things out. Everything was in a state of flux and uncertainty hard to bear. Some of the officers who knew Gipsy's passion for riding lent her their horses, and many a good gallop she had, passing through the dunes covered with coarse, bent grass, beaten down by the wind, out on to the firm, flat sands, where the grey sea frothed and moaned.

One day she was riding with one of the artillery officers, and as she went off full stretch he was left a little behind. All at once he yelled "*Halte!*" with such swift unexpectedness and ferocity that she pulled up sharply, looking behind. "I really thought I must have dropped my horse's tail!"

Amid the immensity of desolate sand walked one simple little lady who was taking an afternoon stroll, and the officer was sitting very erect in his saddle with his hand at the salute. All too late Gipsy gathered that she had ridden at full speed past the noble Queen of the Belgians, of whom it has been said, "She is the greatest heroine in history." It seemed as if Fate was to compel them to miss the queen, and the chagrin was most mortifying.

The Belgian military authorities soon communicated with Mrs. Knocker, and things began to be put on a better footing. The last threads that bound her and Mairi to the ambulance corps, now temporarily at Coxyde, were severed. The Two were officially attached to the Third Division of the Belgian Army. They were asked to continue their work, but at the same time it was announced that no women except these two were to be allowed near the front at all. It was inevitable. The establishment of the *poste* at Pervyse had been the signal for the crowd of sight-seers and those who loved the limelight to dash in and out, often bringing visitors who had nothing whatever to do with ambulance work, but came out of mere curiosity.

Frequently even those who might have helped, instead of setting to work and lending a hand in times of emergency, merely made the tour of the trenches, thereby disturbing everyone and making themselves a nuisance. This could not be permitted any more. The decree went forth, and henceforward Gipsy and her companion were singled out and set apart from all other women in the sight of the army, of which they became a part, and to them alone was accorded this great privilege of remaining in the place of honour and danger. They were asked to establish their *poste* again wherever they thought advisable, and meantime were granted ten days' leave to go over to England to arrange their affairs, and incidentally to collect funds, which were sorely needed.

They might well have used this *congé* for complete rest, but in some ways it was harder than anything they had done yet. Gipsy soon discovered that if she herself could tell the people in England about the work being done, and of the actual state of the case, there was none so mean of soul as to grudge his pence. But the telling was a great strain; to rush about and lecture and allow interviews, which she loathed, tried her sorely.

It was at this time that she focussed into words the idea which had seemed to her more worthwhile doing than anything else in life.

The great object of my work, the theory on which I have been acting and which my experience has proved to be sound, (she says), is the treatment of the wounded for shock before anything else. We have saved many a man who has been brought into my station saying, 'I don't care what you do to my wound; get me warm.' The effects of shock are worse in many cases than the wounds. It is not difficult to imagine it perhaps. When one is under fire, when a shell is coming, one feels like shrivelling up. Even if one is not hit, the effect upon the nervous system is very trying. If a man is hit in such circumstances the effects are much worse.

For a time, some are like mad people. I have known a man wounded, and under ordinary conditions unable to trot, run round and round my dressing-table unable to stop. Another poor fellow, brought in wounded in the lung, was stone grey with cold, unconscious, and apparently lifeless. He was given up as hopeless, and it was said that if an attempt were made to get him back to the hospital he would certainly die on the road. I got him in front of the fire, wrapped him in hot blankets, applied hot-water bottles, rubbed his extremities, and got him warm. After two hours' work he roused up and asked for a drink. That man is now convalescent in a hospital in England, and is expecting to go back to the front. That is one case out of many.

The object of my dressing-station, situated as near as I can possibly get it to the trenches, is to provide a place of rest for the wounded. They are made comfortable and warm, and given some hours' rest, before being joggled over the rough Belgian roads to the hospitals where their hurts can be attended to. If the wounded soldiers can rest out of the trenches before being treated they recover quicker. In the ordinary way, the wounded remain in the trenches until night, when the military ambulances can be brought up for them. Our work is to get them out of the trenches as soon after they are hit as possible.

No wonder all those who heard her story were melted by it, and money came in rapidly—at any rate, rapidly enough for the little they needed. Lord Norreys gave an ambulance car, a 16-20 h.p. Wolseley, which had been presented to the St. John Ambulance Association by Sutton Coldfield and district. This did the most wonderful work described later. With two hundred pounds in hand, the Two returned to Pervyse full of cheer. They were proud and pleased to find themselves for the first time beyond the hand-to-mouth state they had always hitherto existed in, and knowing how far they could make the money go, they felt quite rich and above the possibility of want for some time to come.

They were once more in Belgium before the end of March, and began to look about for a lodging. Naturally they returned to Pervyse, which had so strong a hold on their affections. Just outside the village, farther out than the poor ruined *génie* house, was a little place called the Villa Espagnole, which it seemed to them might be made to do. It was in a filthy state, but that was easily remedied. Mairi started at once to scrub it with that thoroughness characteristic of her, while Gipsy went into La Panne to fetch out the possessions they had left there. But all the time Mairi scrubbed she felt uncomfortable; there was something lonesome and decayed about that villa, an awful smell of the dead, and more than once she got up and went outside to draw in a long breath of the clean air before getting on with her natural vigour.

Directly Gipsy returned with the pots and pans she had to go out again to retrieve a wounded man, and she was away a long time. Dusk began to gather, and with it there crept up like a thickening fog this eerie feeling that could no longer be ignored. Least imaginative of persons, there is yet in Mairi that vein of "second sight" so often found in her countrymen, and an audible voice whispered softly to her in warning:

Take care; leave this place; you mustn't stay here.

So strong did the obsession become that she left off trying to do anything and went outside, preferring to wait in the road, though it was now pitch dark, until Gipsy came back.

The villa was very small. It consisted only of two downstairs rooms and one upstairs. There were two or three steps down to the road, and these opened directly from the principal room. This room itself communicated with the kitchen at the back by another two steps, and from it also a stairway led up to the room above. Beneath this stairway was a third door, bolted and barred, which gave access to some cellar or underground place.

Mairi stood at the foot of the front steps in the road until she heard the welcome sound of the returning car. The wounded man was

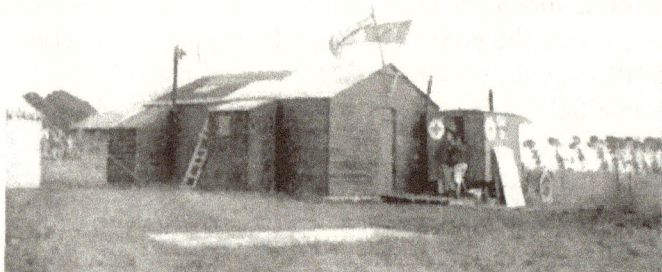

THE STEENKERKE HUT.

FIELD-KITCHEN AND CAR.

The general's son

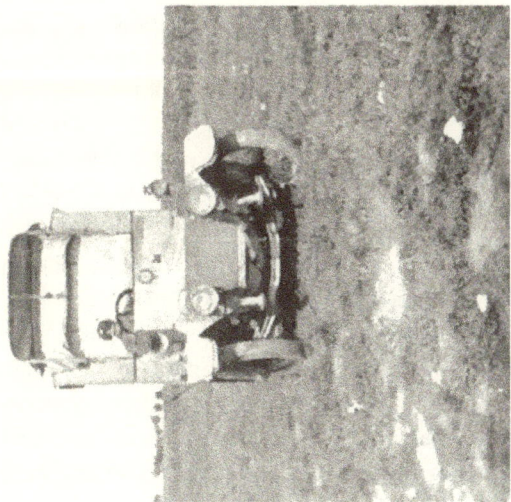

Mrs. Knocker drives the wonderful Wolseley ambulance.

bound up and sent back to La Panne in charge of the chauffeur, who presently returned.

The fire burnt cheerfully enough that evening as they ate their simple supper of bread and butter, but though Mairi naturally said nothing about her odd feelings, Gipsy got up once or twice and moved uneasily round like a dog or a cat in a new house, and even while she was sitting her eyes roved about disquietingly.

They had thrown down plenty of straw in one corner and laid their two sleeping-bags upon it, and in another corner there was straw for the new chauffeur, Augustus, who had superseded Tom, required for duty elsewhere. They called him Augustus for the all-sufficient reason that he "looked like it."

The fire was still well alight when they tucked up in their sleeping-bags for the night, but it did not seem to produce any warmth. There was a chill as of death in the air, and the "something" kept on its almost audible whisper, "Go away, go away." At last even matter-of-fact Mairi could bear it no longer, and creeping nearer to her friend she felt for her hand.

"What is it ?" asked Gipsy, startled.

"Gipsy, there is something dead in here; but—yet—it's—not—dead—"

Gipsy sat upright suddenly. "I haven't dared to tell you," she said. "But ever since I have been in this house something has been saying quite distinctly in my ear, 'Go,' and it makes me feel cold all over. But, Mairi, it isn't real cold; it's a queer kind of cold that never gets warm—any—more—"

They had spoken in whispers, but suddenly the chauffeur sat up and said in French, "*Il y a quelque chose de je ne sais quoi*—"

They were not apt to suffer from nerves, those three; they had seen death too often and in too many horrid forms to be scared by it, but now they knew it was something beyond death that had awed them, something which was vague and terrible, and to all three it seemed as if this "thing" was behind that rusty barred door. It was imprisoned, yet menacing, and was trying intangibly to thrust them away.

They did not sleep at all for the remainder of the night, and were glad when the morning dawned. Without consulting each other, they had simultaneously made up their minds that this house was impossible, and as soon as they could they went to Headquarters and stated that it was unsatisfactory, without giving reasons, and asked for suggestions as to settling elsewhere.

Afterwards there came rumours of the strange influence of that house on others besides themselves. A priest had been living there, and was unable to move because his military duties tied him to the place, and there was no habitable corner elsewhere in it. From the first he had felt uncomfortable, but had struggled against the nameless horror that crept into his veins, and in the end he had gone mad with it!

CHAPTER 14

The Steenkerke Hut

As there were no other houses that could be inhabited in Pervyse, and, furthermore, as, even if there had been, there was no manner of use exposing wounded men to the dangers of that much shelled place, it was decided that a hut must be put up some way back from Pervyse for the sole purpose of the *poste*. As the Two had now a banking account, and were in consequence feeling free to do what they thought best, they talked it over with Mr. Costa, Harrod's representative, who was then doing some hospital-building at La Panne. He entered into their plans warmly, and brushing aside obstacles set to work at once. For the week during which the little hut was being constructed the Two lodged in La Panne.

The hut was put together in the manner of the prairie huts of Canada, and, when ready, was carted up on huge army lorries and put in position in a field just off the road away back from Pervyse toward Furnes. It will be seen from the map that Avecappelle and Steenkerke lie just off this road about half-way between Furnes and Pervyse. The hut was not far from Avecappelle. In the nature of the case there could be no cellar, but as it was supposed to be out of the fire-zone that did not matter.

The Two finally took possession on Wednesday, April 11, when two sick men were sent to them. They revelled in the cleanliness and the newness of the hut after the constant smell of mortar and dust which they had breathed in the thickened air so long. Gipsy writes:

I wish I could show you our funny little wooden house. It is like a Canadian log-hut, and contains two fair-sized rooms, one for ourselves and one for the sick and wounded; and two wee cubicles, one for the orderly and one for our stores, dressings, etc. We have the motor-kitchen drawn up tight against our door, and we step out sideways into it. There we make soup for the soldiers and do our sick-room cookery. The work here is more tiring than it was at Pervyse, because we take both sick and wounded, and that makes more cooking; but I love it all, and only long to be able to keep it going.

But, alas! they were not destined to be free from trouble.

About six o'clock on Sunday, 14th, only three days after they had finally got straight, Mairi was writing out accounts in one room and Gipsy was massaging a patient in the other, the whole of the five available beds being occupied by wounded men. Suddenly a sound they never thought of hearing there shrieked into their ears, and "out of the nowhere" arrived a huge shell, which came down somewhere quite near with a thunderous crash. The noise and force of it, shaking the ground like an earthquake, told their experienced ears that it must be a twenty-one centimetre shell, commonly called a *vingt-et-un*; and this was dropping near a little wooden shed with a match-boarding roof which would not have stopped for the fraction of a second a 7.5 centimetre shell! Gipsy's face expressed all she felt; she was white with horror at the thought of the *blessés* lying there in her charge. She flew to help them on with their clothes, and bundled them out of the house into a little stone house; then, dashing out on to the road, she hailed a passing motor-bike, seated herself on the carrier, and went thus to Steenkerke to fetch the Wolseley ambulance, which was on duty there.

Mairi, who had not for one instant lost her steadiness, waited until the last man cleared the door, and then locked up. Francois, a new orderly who had been lent to them by the army, stayed with her, and when they came round the corner of the house the others had vanished. The first shell had been quickly followed by many similar ones, and they were now simply raining round. It was not safe to go upon the road, which is usually more shelled than anywhere else; besides, if a shell does drop on the hard *pavé*, the resulting explosion from the impact is so terrific that there would be nothing left of anyone within a wide radius. Knowing this, Mairi cut across the fields, with Francois at her heels, but they had the most awful time of their lives, and it took them half an hour to traverse one small field! When they heard the murderous shriek they went flat on their faces in the mud, and waited for the final explosion, and then got up and ran a few feet and dropped again. Sometimes, even as they ran, the force of an explosion threw them down.

The air was literally humming with shells. But even in her bewilderment Mairi noticed the curious clean scoop they make in the soft mud of a field, like an inverted funnel or a wine-glass, with the sides as smooth as paste so different from the jagged, broken craters of the smashed roads. Once, as she lay there, expecting every instant she would be wiped out of material existence, she put out her hand mechanically to touch the fragment of a shell which had fallen beside her, and started to feel it burning hot. Another most odd fact was that the larks were singing all the time. They almost seemed to like the noise, and in every tiny scrap of silence their notes rose high and clear. The whole effect was awesome, like some weird dream.

When they finally got on to the Steenkerke Road they were out of range, but where was Gipsy? Hardly had the question arisen when she appeared with the Wolseley ambulance. She had come back to look for them, and was thankful beyond words that they were safe. Her fine sense of responsibility had made her put in safety first of all the wounded who were in her charge, but the instant they were disposed of she had sought for her friend.

All thoughts of remaining in a hut in that position was at an end. When the shelling quieted down a little later on they returned and collected some of their belongings, and, after talking the matter over together, asked Mr. Costa to put up the hut for them again nearer Steenkerke.

Three times they had been shelled out of their refuges and escaped unhurt. What would the end be?

The building of the hut had made a big hole in the funds collected for the upkeep of the *poste*, and its removal was a disaster, because it necessitated further inroads on their small capital. However, they were not to be daunted, and with the hut once more set up the work began again.

They were certainly much better off in many ways than they had ever been before. Here, besides the five beds for soldiers, there was one in a separate room for an officer. They were well provided with cars. Mairi, who has a head for detail, gives an exact list of them:

"A 16-20 h.p. Wolseley ambulance (St. John Ambulance car), a 75 h.p. Mércèdes, and a 40-60 Fiat with a kitchen body."

Besides these, the British Red Cross had given them a lorry for fetching goods from Dunkirk, but it was "such a beast" that they ex-

COUNT DE GRUNNE AND MAJOR A. A. GORDON, M.V.O.

VISITORS (BARON HAROLD DE T'SERCLAES IN THE CENTRE).

Paul the Chauffeur

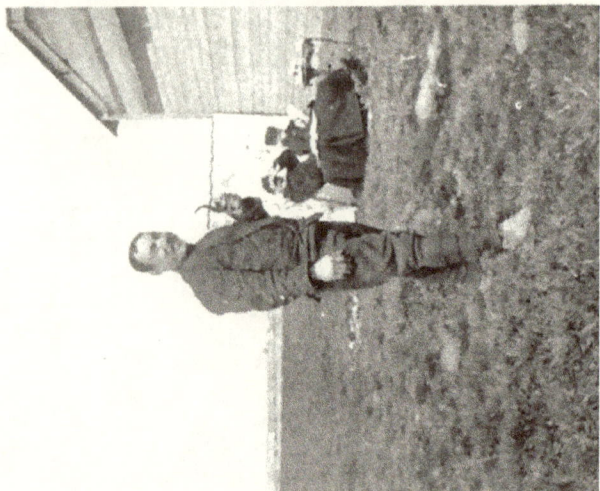

François the Orderly

changed it for a "dear little 10-12 h.p. Mors," which did excellent work.

★★★★★★

The first officer to occupy the small room was the son of General Jacquez, and his being entrusted to their care was felt to be a mark of great confidence. Rumour at once rolled around. "It was the son of a General they had in charge. What General? Oh, General French, of course. No, it was a royalty. Then it must be Prince Alexander of Teck." And so on. All these surmises and conjectures reached their ears from time to time, and caused them much amusement.

From this time the *poste* took on a more established character. Mrs. Knocker appealed for cards, puzzles, French books, chocolate, and cigarettes for her beloved wounded.

> It is such a splendid little country! (she said.) I have lived amongst the soldiers so long, and know how plucky and cheerful they are. I see them patched up, returning to their regiments unmurmuring. I wonder if even our British Tommy would fight so cheerfully as he does if he were established on twenty miles of Kent, knowing that all the rest of his country was in the hands of the Germans, not knowing where his mother, wife, or sisters were, or if he would ever see them again. What awful odds against them! I am asking for funds to enable me to keep up my little hospital, and not give up the work I am so keen about.

Rations were supplied by the army for each wounded soldier, but they needed more than that to feed them up. Also there was no allowance of food for the ladies themselves, or the orderly and chauffeurs, and coal and other necessaries had to be provided. Even with the utmost economy the cost of running the *poste* was not less than three pounds a week.

One of the most untiring of their friends was Major A. A. Gordon, M.V.O., *Courrier de sa Majesté le Roi des Belges*, who had known them through all their vicissitudes in the Pervyse days, and now continued his visits, never without bringing priceless treasures of condensed milk, preserved *café au lait* and other necessaries.

They had arranged to have stores sent out from Harrods' to Dunkirk once a week, and one of them had to motor in and fetch them. By this time Mairi was quite a good hand at a car, not only at driving it, but in knowing "how to poke her nose inside the bonnet" to make it go when it was sulky.

157

Now that they were not living right up at the trenches, and had their own ambulance, they used to go to collect the wounded. On those open roads they were clearly visible from far away, and the Germans used to make a target of them whenever they saw them. Gipsy draws an amusing little diagram showing the shells marking their course, but always breaking just behind them, so that they look as if the car had dropped them out as it ran.

The Wolseley car, already mentioned as having been presented by Sutton Coldfield and district, did wonderful work. Mairi says of it, "It is a car in a million." Since March, 1915, up to the time of writing, it has carried 1,500 sick and wounded men, and that without any breakdown—a record any car might be proud of. The car has always been driven by one of the Two themselves, and that has helped to keep it in order, for careful driving goes a long way towards the preserving the life of cars, and the way some chauffeurs knock them about is appalling. The experiences of the Two with their various chauffeurs have been painful and amusing together, and the amount of energy expended in the futile hope of keeping some of the men in order is enough to move one to tears.

Gipsy says, "Our cars and our chauffeurs have made us feel older and thinner than any hard work we have ever done." Of course, the first requisite for a driver at the front is pluck, and not only the sort of pluck coming of sound nerves, which almost every chauffeur, even in ordinary home traffic on good roads, must possess, but a kind of dare-devil recklessness in addition. The trouble out there was that if they got a man with this kind of courage, he was as a rule utterly undisciplined, and refused to obey orders, and generally made himself a nuisance. It seemed sometimes as if it were a choice between a polite man who agreed to everything he was told, but simply dropped off the car and sat in a ditch if he approached a tight place, and a reckless, careless, rude fellow who went when he liked and where he liked without the least consideration for what was expected of him.

As an instance of the first type, one day when Mairi was driving up to Pervyse, and reached the long, straight stretch before the village, she found that shells were bursting ahead, but felt she must go on. She continued therefore steadily, but when she reached the village and turned to give an order to the chauffeur Joseph, who should have been seated behind, she found that he had vanished. He had thought it simpler and easier to roll out of the car and lie in the ditch until the danger was over!

In contrast to Joseph there was Paul, who met an order with a dark scowl, and if told to get ready to drive, sometimes replied promptly, "I'm not going to drive this morning," not happening to be in the mood for it. Supposing he were severely reprimanded, he would disappear until he thought his employers had been sufficiently punished. Yet of his pluck there could be no question. He not only went headlong into danger if the mood took him, he really seemed to enjoy it; and if the car broke down he knew every screw and nut in her, and not only could put her right again, but would do it even under fire. Yet at last he got so unbearable that Gipsy asked the general to give him a word of reprimand, thinking innocently that, coming from the general, it must make some impression. When she told her recreant that the general had sent for him at three o'clock, all the reply she got was, "What for?"

She did not give anything away, merely repeating that the general wished to see him, and that he must present himself at Headquarters at three. He answered quite calmly, "Then you can go down and tell the General I'm busy," and departed, hands in pockets, with an expression on his face showing there was no work of any kind to be got out of him for twelve hours; someone had to suffer for their rash interference with his liberty!

This was unbearable, and he had to go, and was replaced by Joseph, whose exploits have been detailed.

Good driving of an ambulance car is not only necessary for preserving the life of the car itself, but the lives of those who are in it. The man who goes fifty miles an hour at and over and into anything, as the Belgian chauffeurs love to do, will probably kill many of those he is carrying, and even if they are not actually murdered, he will cause them unnecessary agony. In driving ambulances holes should be avoided wherever possible, and, even if there is shelling going on, a really good driver will consider his charges and his car rather than his own instinct to get out of it as quickly as possible. Both Gipsy and Mairi thoroughly understand cars, and it is pain and grief to them to hear the gears grate and the nuts wrench and jar by foolish or reckless carelessness. Sometimes Gipsy has been advised, "*Madame*, if you would leave your chauffeurs alone and trust them, they would never give you any trouble."

At last, in desperation, thinking the trouble could not be greater than it was, she did leave them to themselves for one day, with the result that the big 75 h.p. Mércèdes was rushed out to Calais for a joy-ride, and had to be towed back on a lorry because the back axle was smashed! Leaving the chauffeurs alone for a day usually meant a big bill for repairs.

One day the Two were at Oestkerke when the shelling was very hot. Every movement must have been visible to the enemy. They were in the Wolseley ambulance, and turned to the right at some cross-roads and drew up beside a farmhouse. A captain came out from the house and told them there was a wounded man in the village needing them, so they turned and raced back to fetch him under a killing fire. They managed to find him and dashed back, though one shell burst right behind the car. Gipsy, who was in the front seat beside the chauffeur, looked sharply back, expecting to see that the rear part of the car had been sliced off. But for the splendid qualities of the Wolseley car they would never have got out alive, and the Sutton Coldfield donors may feel satisfied that their contributions have achieved notable work. It was for this feat they were mentioned in despatches. The orders of the day ran:

> *J'exprime tous mes remerciements à Madame Knocker et à Mademoiselle Chisholm pour le nouvel acte de dévouement qu'elles ont posé le 25 courant en allant relever un de nos blessés dans une endroit battu par l'artillerie ennémie.*

The general himself came to congratulate them and stayed to have tea.

Money soon began to fail them again, and Gipsy contemplated another run over to England to fill the coffers. It seemed hard that when she was there and able to tell people in person about the work, she should get what she wanted, but the moment she went back to take up the work again subscriptions ceased.

> It seems easy enough to get money, (she says pathetically), when people see you, and hear you talk, and realize what you are doing, but the moment you get back and begin to *do* it again, and cease talking, they forget all about you.

Even though they were now outside the worst danger-zone, they soon realized that it would be the prudent course to bank up the little *poste* with sand-bags to deaden any splinters or shrapnel that might come that way, and Gipsy wrote home praying for bags of any kind, only not too big, because they couldn't lift them themselves. She especially asks that her little son might make one, and have his

THE THIRD POSTS IN PERVYSE.

SAND-BAGS.

THE INSIDE OF THE THIRD HOUSE AS IT WAS FOUND.

THE SAME AS IT WAS MADE.

name painted in large letters across it, so that it might be recognized and could be stuck up in a prominent position. Besides this they had a dugout made beneath the hut into which they could hurry their wounded charges at the first alarm.

The weather had now become very hot. At first this was a welcome change after the long dreary winter, but presently the heat became almost more trying than the cold had been. The glare and dust were awful. But the Two had occasional changes; once one of the naval men took them for a run along the coast in a motor-boat, and the breath of the sea air came like a vivifying blast to both. On another never-to-be-forgotten occasion they went down by invitation to the aviation ground, and there quite suddenly Gipsy found herself being introduced to Baron Harold de T'Serclaes de Rattendael, a representative of one of the oldest Belgian families, and recognized with a quick movement of surprise that this was the officer who had brought messages from his Colonel, and whom she had often thought of since. They had hardly had two words together until then, but the acquaintance formally made seemed as if it were going to blossom. From the very first Mairi, with instinctive tact, always found someone else to talk to at the right moment.

Both the girls were dreadfully tried by that summer. Not for anything would they have given up the work, but yet, "I feel I should love to be quietly at home in a wee cottage with the sound of guns miles away. One gets tired of the same old grind, the same old food, and never a change. I dare not say how sick one gets of it for fear of being disheartened," tells its own tale.

About the end of July, Gipsy visited Pervyse again one day, and discovered how terribly the little *poste* was missed there, so she began to wonder if it would be possible to reopen it. The hut was all very well, but it was not right at the front where the men could get at it any time in coming from the trenches, and the atmosphere of hope and brightness which the mere presence of women had been able to create in the village, was sadly lacking while they were some miles out. There was an empty house opposite the *brasserie* where the officers lived, which, though badly shattered, might perhaps do. She considered the matter, talked it over with the officers, and after a good deal of trouble with Headquarters, gained permission to return there if she wished.

The four outside walls of this "possible" house were still standing, but the roof and inside walls had quite gone, except for two rooms, one of which was the cellar. Mr. Costa put up a wooden partition inside to replace the broken wall, and the Engineers were willing to do all they could, and helped to fix iron rafters across the roof by working at night. They had only just accomplished this when they got orders to move elsewhere. But the two girls, with indomitable pluck and perseverance, themselves dragged up sandbags and piled them on the rafters; and this they did after a heavy day's work at the *poste*, coming up from Steenkerke at nights in order to put it through.

A friend, named Mr. Colby, found them at it one night, and was horrified that they should be using their strength in this rough work. He was most kind, and sent men and materials to the rescue, and it was time someone did, for the heavy work and long strain had had their effect, and Gipsy, who had been showing signs of nerve strain for some time, broke down completely. So both she and Mairi obtained leave, and went over to England. It can hardly be said that this was a holiday any more than the former trip, but at any rate it was change of work; and after lecturing and interviewing, and running about a good deal, they both came back quite well on September 9, 1915.

It was at this time they met again Miss Eva Moore, whom they had worked for when attached to the Women's Emergency Corps. Miss Moore was immensely interested in all they had done since then, and set herself to work untiringly to help them, sending them out funds and contributions in kind which were the greatest help; in fact, had it not been for her, the *poste* might have had to cease altogether.

CHAPTER 15

Enter Romance

The Spirits of the Two rose unaccountably at getting back to Pervyse; Steenkerke had been clean and comfortable, but never could take hold of them as Pervyse had done. Here they had inaugurated the great scheme, here they had worked for months against difficulties. Hungry and cold, and perforce dirty, lacking everything yet doing all things, they had struggled on and been able to perform marvels; their hearts had glowed at the gratitude of the Belgians, their spirits had been cheered by the lively companionship of brave men. They had their ups and downs, and, as was inevitable, all had not been quite smooth sailing between them, but each slight "breeze" had left their deep friendship for each other deeper than before, as they felt how necessary they were to each other.

It was more than a year since they had come out, two members of a comparatively large band, ignorant of what would be expected of them, and unable to give effect to what they felt might be done arid ought to be done. They had evolved this scheme and carried it through against opposition and difficulty which in these pages have been only faintly indicated; sometimes it had seemed as if they must be overwhelmed and let go, but always doggedly they had held on, and now they had emerged on to what seemed by contrast tolerably firm ground.

From the cramped and stuffy cellar-house they had mounted to the shot-torn *génie*. Thence they had passed to the clean little newly built, and in some ways convenient, hut, but it had not held for them the homeliness they found in the desolate village of Pervyse.

Mr. Colby had been as good or better than his word; when they came back after their holiday, full of eagerness, they found that the ceiling of the bedroom had been laid a foot thick in concrete and

165

piled up with sand-bags. The other rooms were still unfinished, but they set gaily to work to splash about whitewash with energy, and to make the great red crosses outside to signify their merciful work. The bedroom and living-room in this house looked out over the street, and at the back were the *blessé* room and the cellar Mairi ought to have been an engineer or architect, for she adorns her journal all the way through with little ground-plans, showing the arrangement of the rooms in all their abodes, and never seems satisfied until this is done. She was full of enthusiasm about the new house; it was at the same time an "abode of bliss," and "not such a bad little hole considering all things."

The *brasserie* was exactly opposite, and the men of the regiment gave the Two a rousing welcome; they did not seem in the least surprised that *Les Dames Anglaises* had been unable to live far from them, and had felt impelled to come back again. There was so much to do to the house that they had not got it exactly as they wished until three months had passed. During this time they had more than one bombardment. One day it was very hot with 15-centimetre shells, which fell all around them and the *brasserie*, which was pierced in several places, one shell actually going down into the cellar there and wounding three men. A call was made for help, and the Two dashed across the road in the thick of the falling shells to do the bandaging. They had not lost any of their *élan* through familiarity with danger. They used the little hut near Steenkerke as an evacuation station, and took the wounded out there at once. The kind of incident that came very frequently into their lives at this time is best told in Gipsy's own words:

I had just come back from taking three badly sick men to Steenkerke Infirmary, and was tidying up, when the sudden distant boom of a German gun was heard, so quickly followed by the hasty shriek and the crash of explosion. I wondered why I had managed to get in just in time, and why Mairi and I had not been outside, as we so often are—our luck is so kind to us. This one shell was followed by the usual succession; I was glad we had a fortified dugout, and that we were fairly safe.

Suddenly a little soldier came to our open door and told me, with tears in his eyes, that a comrade had been terribly badly injured, and they were bringing him to me. I hurriedly dragged out the wheels of the running stretcher, and he ran up the road,

The nave of the ruined church
at Pervyse.

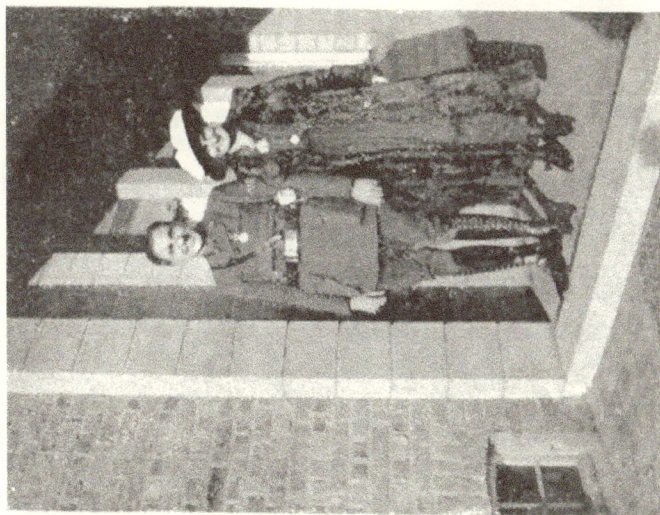

The baron and baroness
on their weddind day.

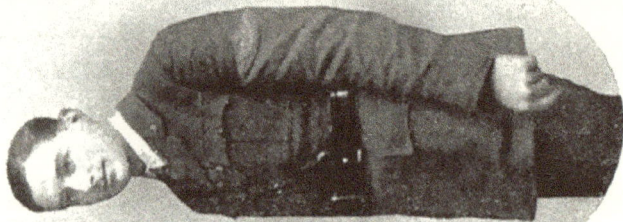

Baron Harold de T'Serclaes

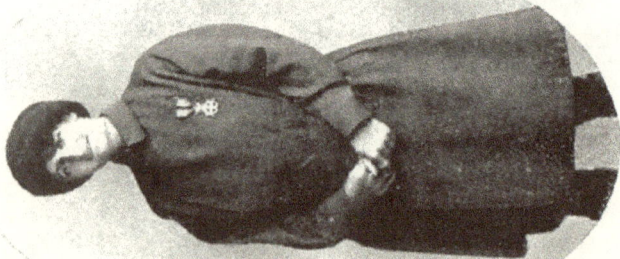

Baroness Harold de T'Serclaes

while I prepared the room and got all possible quick dressings ready. When this was done I went out to meet the stretcher, and I saw at once that the poor brave little soldier was past my aid. I said to them, '*Il est mort.*' They turned to me with an incredible look, as if I had spoken from inexperience, but I have seen so many—the number runs into thousands—that I could make no mistake. Poor comrades! they looked so sad and heartbroken; he was obviously a favourite. I ordered the stretcher to be taken to the garage—or, rather, what we call the garage—a tumbled-down outhouse, where stands our emergency car. Had this man had the remotest chance of life I should have, within five minutes, placed him in the car *en route* for La Panne. Poor man! it seemed so sad, and one cannot help asking, 'Why?'— why should it be he, and not Mairi or I? Here was a laughing, cheerful, healthy man one short quarter of an hour ago, and now still and silent, and past all pain.

His friends kept asking if I was *sure* he was dead. Was it possible to live with his terrible wound? A bit of shell had taken off half his head. I turned and asked a soldier to see if there was a doctor in the place, just to write out his paper; but, as is so often the case, there was no doctor: it was '*Madame*' who had to do all the last little rites, so Mairi and I set to work to search his pockets— such a pathetic work, it brings one so much in touch with Life and its meaning. Just a few scraps of paper, containing a few words of happiness from friends or relatives, a tobacco-box, a pipe, his *plaque d'identité*, and a gold ring on his finger.

His friends tell me his brother is at Avecappelle, and would like to have everything, even the ring, so it must be taken off—it is so tight and so difficult to get off. I put everything together in a little pile—such a little pile—and cross his arms upon his chest, and cover him with a rug. How I hate the look of those silent, humpy stretchers—and the thoughts keep racing through my mind, and I know by Mairi's face she is thinking the same! 'Why?' and 'I wonder'; and it gives one a longing to be miles away from this war.

As the batteries are silent and the road is clear and there is a long way to go, I have that stretcher placed in the car, and Mairi and I drive it to the cemetery at Adinkerke. There it is put on the long clean table, and measured for the coffin. We drive away once more for Pervyse, feeling weary of heart and sad. All along we meet the little soldiers who greet us with a cheer, and we have to force a smile in response.

But it was not all depressing, for they had many true and staunch friends who came in to see them, and the brightness of both officers and men was extraordinary. A new joy also had entered into Gipsy's life, for every now and again, when the weather was too bad for any flying to be possible, the young Baron H. de T'Serclaes appeared at Pervyse, and his wonderful smile irradiated the most dismal day. In November, one day when Mairi as usual had discreetly absented herself to fulfil some household jobs, he proposed and was accepted! On talking it over the happy pair agreed (according to the usual custom on such occasions) that they would not be married for a long time. In their case there certainly seemed to be some reason, and they decided to wait until the end of the War. But the self-denying ordinance was about as lasting as it generally is in such cases, and as the days went on and love grew apace, they found the extreme difficulty of being engaged in anything like a satisfactory manner amid such extreme publicity, and began to waver.

Of course it was quite possible to argue the matter both ways; the fact that they were in danger of their lives every day seemed to urge upon them the common sense of getting married at once, and making the best of what time might be left to them. This view was especially predominant when, after a long ride over execrable roads in abominable weather, the young baron found himself discussing such subjects as the gramophone, the cars, and other superficial things during his short time off, and even this had to be carried on in gulps because of the incessant inroads of soldiers, chauffeurs, and every imaginable kind of "other," none of whom possessed the tact of Mairi. Gipsy suggests that it is a test of true love, whether it will stand this most aggravating experience, with the addition of continual bursts of huge shells banging overhead, draughts wreathing round one's feet, and perpetual small worries to improve one's temper.

It was before Christmas that the idea, fostered by such influences, finally won the day, and it was decided they were to be married in January, 1916.

To Mairi, of course, this would make an enormous change; never again would she have her friend entirely to herself, and the good days in which they had grown to know each other in all sorts of circumstances were over.

But though Mairi felt the separation bitterly she was far too loyal to do other than rejoice in her friend's happiness, and even her private diary contains nothing but pleasure at this unexpected change.

Except for the visits of "Harry," that winter was a very quiet one in Pervyse. The place was more desolate than ever. The year before, the houses, though ruined, were mostly standing, now many more were heaps of stones, without a suggestion of life. Previously horses had been quartered in some of the sheds, the Engineer officers had been coming and going, "one saw movement"; even in the village there were usually soldiers marching to or from the trenches, and when the first shells fell after an interval, there had often been a rush for shelter like that of rabbits flying to their holes in a warren on the approach of a "human." But this year there was hardly a living being to be seen; the only inhabited place besides the *poste* was the *brasserie*.

If one walks through the village one sees nothing but absolute ruin and desolation. Poor little Pervyse! The Germans certainly have knocked it about. In the Rue de Dixmude the houses which are left are crumbling to pieces, soon there won't be even an upstanding wall left. The Hôtel de Ville is most depressing, it lifts one great chimney to the sky, the other long since having fallen, and on one wall in the interior, which is now laid bare, is the figure of an angel. The weather has been awful, all through these months, rain falling unceasingly. Our shelter is filled with water, and we are obliged to pump it out frequently.

As far as the rest went it was all much the same; the great artillery duels raged overhead, shells fell around, and many wounded were brought in.

Our work comprises every kind of thing. Now that the winter months are in full swing the men need much attention if they are to be kept alive. Woollen garments of every sort are in great demand. Often men come to us soaked through from head to foot, having fallen into the inundations while doing patrol work, and then we are able to give them a place to themselves where they can undress and wrap themselves up in blankets, while their clothes are being dried in the oven. We attend to all their wants: cuts, burns, sore feet, boils, all kinds of little ailments which a doctor cannot, or will not, be bothered with.

The Two still carried out hot drinks at night to the sentinels at the *avant-poste*, and still made soup and cocoa for the hungry, cold men in the trenches. Their faithful friend, Robert de Wilde, who had become like an elder brother, dropped in frequently in the evenings, but there were not many others.

So the time passed on until January. The day for the great event was fixed for the nineteenth, and there was much to arrange first.

It seemed as if everyone had to give their permission, (says Gipsy). The man sends in his demand to get married, and with it his *fiancée's* birth certificate, and an account of her parents, stating whether they are of good family or not. Then the round begins. This goes to the Commandant; he considers it and signs it. He sends it on to the Commanding Officer of the Aviation, who does the same. From there it goes to General Headquarters. From there to the Ministry. From there to the War Minister. From there to the King. Then it reverses the route and crawls back again.

The ceremony was to take place in La Panne from the little villa which the Two had occupied in their last week there together, and two days before it, Gipsy was there arranging matters when up came Baron Harold de T'Serclaes laughing, and said the papers had indeed at last returned from their long journey, but there was no birth certificate with them; it had been dropped apparently somewhere on the way, and the Tribunal refused to go through with the marriage unless it turned up!

And this at the eleventh hour, when all the guests were invited!

What could I do? (says the poor bride-to-be). I sat down and racked my brains. There seemed no two ways open to me. I could wire to my wonderful shipping agent in Dover, who has so many times pulled me through difficulties, and ask him to send someone to London by passenger train to Somerset House, there to get a duplicate of the certificate, and with it catch the Calais boat the following day, so that he could hand the certificate to the Captain, arid I would meet the boat at this end and get it from him. But all this would take a lot of explaining in a wire, and involved a fearful risk, as things might go wrong.

Secondly, I might go to Havre and myself fetch the missing certificate, which must be there. But Havre is a seven-hour journey by road, and is outside the zone of my pass—that left me only one day to get a *laissez-passer*—and supposing I allowed for a fifteen-hour journey, I could only just do it without counting any breakdowns. What a position! I saw my wedding-day vanishing into dim mists, but as my *fiancé* was being cheery I was going to be so too, and I did not let him see how dreadfully worrying all this was to me. I crawled back to Pervyse that night, still beating my brains to find a way out. There I found the *poste* full of sick and wounded, and so much work to do that I had not time to think even about my own wedding.

But in the middle of the night a thought flashed upon me that I had with me an old tin box full of papers, and in among them all my hospital examination papers, and I had had to have a birth certificate to get into the hospital, so it might be there still.

It was!

So the ceremony had not to be postponed, after all!

It had been suggested that the marriage might take place in the ruined church of Pervyse, open to the sky, where there was still a bit of the altar standing, but, used as she was to continuing her work calmly amid falling shells, Gipsy considered that in such conditions her responses might not be so clear and firm as she would wish, and also that the coming and going of such a party of people might draw the German fire, arid so the idea was set aside.

January 18 was a Tuesday, and on the evening of that day Mairi writes:

> The day before THE DAY! How strange it seems that the dear kid is going to get married! We have so often talked about it and discussed it laughingly, and now it is going to become fact. How things change! The last day I shall ever have Winkles to myself! (Winkles was another pet name evolved spontaneously.) Pray God she may be happy! She deserves happiness, if anyone does. Dear little Winkles, what a good friend you have been to me! You will never realize what it has meant to me to be with you for these months. I shall miss you horribly. Goodbye, Winkles; good luck to you, and all my very best wishes for your future life.

Captain Robert de Wilde, who was to be best man, turned up early and had breakfast with them. Gipsy says of him:

> One of the most charming and bravest of the Belgian officers

I have met. We have shared the ups and downs of shelling ever since the first days of Pervyse, when he was observation officer. He is now in command of a battery. He talks English as we do, and is one of those rare men who are always cheerful.

They started in the Wolseley car at eight o'clock, and no sooner had they got clear of the village than Gipsy remembered she had left her shoes behind, and had to go back. Lucky that she wasn't caught by a shell. She was dressed for the wedding in a blue frock and a big black hat, with a white wing across the front—very suitable in view of the bridegroom's position. They arrived at the villa which had been lent to them about 9.30, and there the bridegroom met them for the civil ceremony. Then they went on to the church, a Roman Catholic chapel, which faith the bride had embraced before her marriage.

The organ was beautifully played during the ceremony, and the congregation rivalled that to be found at any West End London church at a society wedding.

There were present Brigadier-General Prince Alexander of Teck, the Russian representative, General Jacquez, Lady Denbigh and her two daughters, one of whom—Lady Dorothie—had played her part in the ambulance work, Baron de Bleaumaerts, Baron de Wahliss, many of the officers of the Belgian Army, and personal friends. Even the photographers were not omitted, and the war-wedding was quite like those usually known in peace.

With this the book might end, as 80 *per cent*, of the reading public consider a wedding the only satisfactory conclusion, but there is still something to say. Mairi went over with the happy pair on leave to England. She obtained permission, after exceeding difficulty, for her father to come and share her rough and dangerous life at Pervyse. She was back at her post before the honeymooners, and went down to Boulogne to welcome them on their return on February 8. Then she performed the really amazing feat for a girl of her age (she was by this time close on twenty) of driving them back from Boulogne to La Panne and taking the car on to Pervyse, altogether 160 miles!

The *poste* was further fortified by endless sand-bags and made more secure. But the question of means continued to be an anxious one. When Gipsy resumed her work she and Mairi discussed it often. They realized that they could not continue to draw from the few personal friends, who had already given as much as they could possibly afford, yet how were they to reach a larger public? One day, when the question was to the fore, someone said to them that if only means could be found of letting the general public in England know what they had done and were still doing, he was sure many, many people would gladly subscribe, a view that seemed borne out by the ready way which money flowed in if one of the hard workers themselves told the people of England of their life. It was suggested, therefore, that their cherished diaries, which they had kept entirely for their own interest, should be handed over to someone they knew, who had the requisite knowledge of the conditions, to be written out in book form, and then they should be published.

Thus the wider public—that which reads—might be reached, in which case it would be easy to ask everyone who sympathized with the work to send some trifle, even if only a shilling, after reading the book. Many shillings would fill the exchequer. After some persuasion this was agreed to. The Two had always hated publicity, but owing to the unique character of their work and the approval of the King of the Belgians, they had not been altogether able to hide their light under a bushel, as they would have preferred to; so for the sake of that work, which was their very life, they agreed to go further, and with pain and grief handed over the journals to see what could be made of them.

Mairi is still hard at work, and Gipsy is still as devoted as ever, despite her new responsibilities.

On March 2, 1916, in the early morning a message came to them that King Albert was going to visit the trenches at Pervyse, and would probably look in at the *poste* on the way. Luckily Gipsy had been staying there for the night, so she was on the spot, and able to help Mairi to tidy up with all speed. The dugout looked very dusty and sombre when they viewed it to see if it was fit for the king, but they had done all that was possible.

As early as 8.15 the king came down the village street accompanied by two generals; he was dressed in khaki, with a khaki metal helmet on his head, and looked taller than ever among those gaunt ruins. The Two stood by the door of the *poste* to see him go by, and when his eye fell on them he came across to them and held out his hand in a friendly way.

"I want to congratulate you on all you are doing for my soldiers," he said. "I think you are very courageous to stay up here."

Glowingly they replied that they loved their work more than ever; it had become a part of them.

"I hope you are sufficiently sheltered ?" he asked, glancing at the piled-up sandbags.

Yes, indeed, they assured him. Would he care to look inside? So he lifted his helmet and, stooping, came in.

Now among the most valuable possessions of the *poste* was a Siamese kitten, which had been given to the Two, and which was never allowed to stray into the street, lest its small life should be abruptly ended. With the usual propensity of its species, its one endeavour was always to get out, and whenever the door of the dugout was opened from outside, those coming in put down a wary hand and stopped its tumultuous exit. In this case, however, neither of the Two could go in before the king, and they looked at each other as the door opened. The orderly, Henri, who had been with them for a long time, and loved them and all things that were theirs, including the kitten, with deep devotion, seeing the door open and the kitten make a bolt, flew from the innermost recesses, crying out:

"*Hélas! Attention la, que le petit chat ne se sauve pas!*" Thus he came right up against the king! Poor man, he looked as if he would never get over it!

The king only laughed as the *petit chat* was frustrated, and looking round the low room with interest, he noted the portraits of himself and the queen and their family hanging on the walls, doubtless remembering that Gipsy was now legally his own subject.

When he turned to go he thanked them again in a simple, friendly way, and asked how long they had been in Pervyse.

When they told him, he echoed, "Eighteen months! It is a long time," and with a kindly hand-clasp he passed on.

Baroness de T'Serclaes said at her recent public meetings in England:

> I found that far too many of the stretchers contained dead bodies when they arrived at the base hospital, and it seemed to me that the reason must be that they had died from shock or from the way they were driven over the badly-shelled roads. I appealed to the Belgian Government, and asked if they would permit Miss Chisholm and myself to go into the trenches and try and see if, by treating the soldiers for shock at once, we could save life.
>
> After several refusals we were allowed to go into the trenches for twenty-four hours, and have stayed nearly two years.
>
> In March, 1915, when the big war conference was held in Paris,

and it was decided that no women were to be permitted in the trenches at all, it was further decided, after examining the work I and Miss Chisholm were doing, that we should be the only two women who were permitted in the firing-line, because our treatment was necessary. I found it was as I thought, and if one could get to a soldier directly he was hit, and treat him for shock, he was able to stand an operation better than one who was bundled into an ambulance and driven quickly over bad roads to the operating-table, where he, perhaps, died under the operation or from the after effects. . . . We are in telephonic communication with every trench in the division, and have many thousand men to look after. The telephone means that when a man wants our care we can get to him right away. We do all we can to save the men's lives, and on many occasions we are able to deal with them so quickly that they are on the operating-table within twenty minutes!

And even after the war, when Belgium comes into her own again, the work will not cease; there will be crippled men, and helpless men, and men wholly incapable of doing anything for themselves: these will all need care and attention, and in her new country the Baroness will find ample work to fill her life in devoting herself to the "splendid little Belgian soldiers" whom she has learned to love.

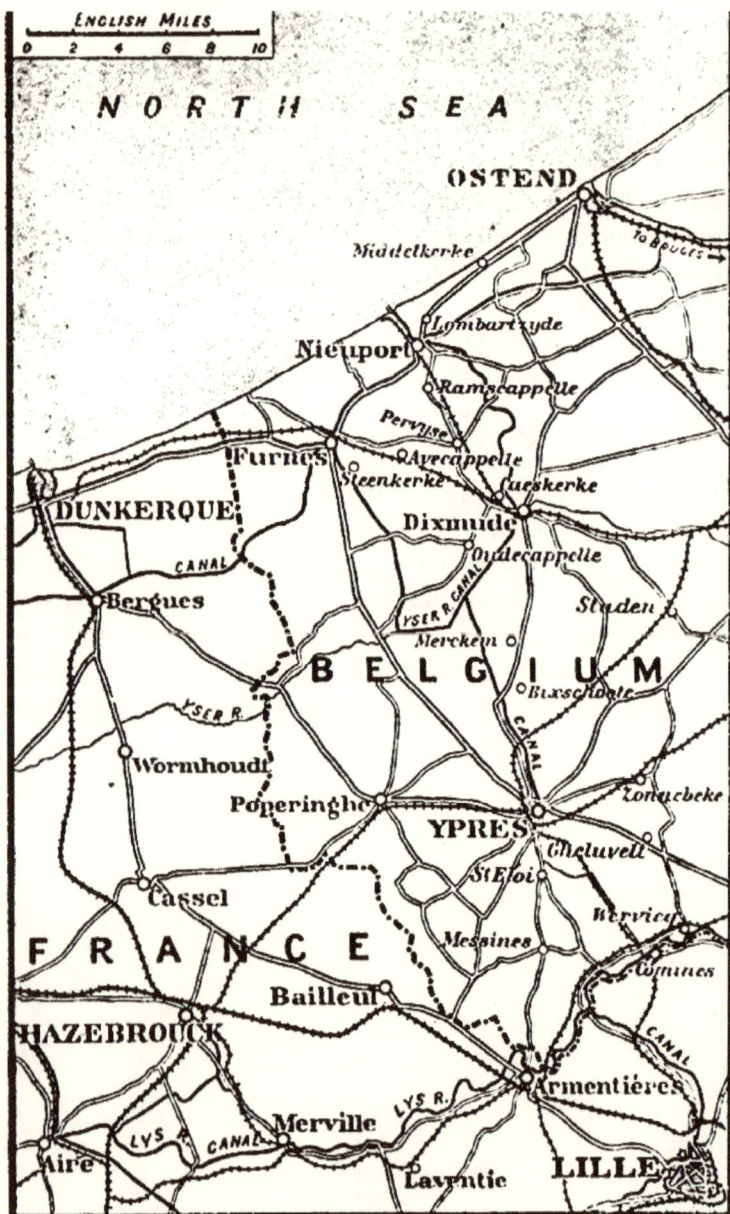

SKETCH-MAP OF THE DISTRICT ROUND PERVYSE.

LEONAUR

ALSO FROM LEONAUR
AVAILABLE IN SOFTCOVER OR HARDCOVER WITH DUST JACKET

THE WOMAN IN BATTLE by Loreta Janeta Velazquez—Soldier, Spy and Secret Service Agent for the Confederacy During the American Civil War.

BOOTS AND SADDLES by Elizabeth B. Custer—The experiences of General Custer's Wife on the Western Plains.

FANNIE BEERS' CIVIL WAR by Fannie A. Beers—A Confederate Lady's Experiences of Nursing During the Campaigns & Battles of the American Civil War.

LADY SALE'S AFGHANISTAN by Florentia Sale—An Indomitable Victorian Lady's Account of the Retreat from Kabul During the First Afghan War.

THE TWO WARS OF MRS DUBERLY by Frances Isabella Duberly—An Intrepid Victorian Lady's Experience of the Crimea and Indian Mutiny.

THE REBELLIOUS DUCHESS by Paul F. S. Dermoncourt—The Adventures of the Duchess of Berri and Her Attempt to Overthrow French Monarchy.

LADIES OF WATERLOO by Charlotte A. Eaton, Magdalene de Lancey & Juana Smith—The Experiences of Three Women During the Campaign of 1815: Waterloo Days by Charlotte A. Eaton, A Week at Waterloo by Magdalene de Lancey & Juana's Story by Juana Smith.

NURSE AND SPY IN THE UNION ARMY by Sarah Emma Evelyn Edmonds—During the American Civil War

WIFE NO. 19 by Ann Eliza Young—The Life & Ordeals of a Mormon Woman During the 19th Century

DIARY OF A NURSE IN SOUTH AFRICA by Alice Bron—With the Dutch-Belgian Red Cross During the Boer War

MARIE ANTOINETTE AND THE DOWNFALL OF ROYALTY by Imbert de Saint-Amand—The Queen of France and the French Revolution

THE MEMSAHIB & THE MUTINY by R. M. Coopland—An English lady's ordeals in Gwalior and Agra duringthe Indian Mutiny 1857

MY CAPTIVITY AMONG THE SIOUX INDIANS by Fanny Kelly—The ordeal of a pioneer woman crossing the Western Plains in 1864

WITH MAXIMILIAN IN MEXICO by Sara Yorke Stevenson—A Lady's experience of the French Adventure

LEONAUR

ALSO FROM LEONAUR
AVAILABLE IN SOFTCOVER OR HARDCOVER WITH DUST JACKET

A DIARY FROM DIXIE *by Mary Boykin Chesnut*—A Lady's Account of the Confederacy During the American Civil War

FOLLOWING THE DRUM *by Teresa Griffin Vielé*—A U. S. Infantry Officer's Wife on the Texas frontier in the Early 1850's

FOLLOWING THE GUIDON *by Elizabeth B. Custer*—The Experiences of General Custer's Wife with the U. S. 7th Cavalry.

LADIES OF LUCKNOW *by G. Harris & Adelaide Case*—The Experiences of Two British Women During the Indian Mutiny 1857. A Lady's Diary of the Siege of Lucknow by G. Harris, Day by Day at Lucknow by Adelaide Case

MARIE-LOUISE AND THE INVASION OF 1814 *by Imbert de Saint-Amand*— The Empress and the Fall of the First Empire

SAPPER DOROTHY *by Dorothy Lawrence*—The only English Woman Soldier in the Royal Engineers 51st Division, 79th Tunnelling Co. during the First World War

ARMY LETTERS FROM AN OFFICER'S WIFE 1871-1888 *by Frances M. A. Roe*—Experiences On the Western Frontier With the United States Army

NAPOLEON'S LETTERS TO JOSEPHINE *by Henry Foljambe Hall*—Correspondence of War, Politics, Family and Love 1796-1814

MEMOIRS OF SARAH DUCHESS OF MARLBOROUGH, AND OF THE COURT OF QUEEN ANNE VOLUME 1 by A. T. Thomson

MEMOIRS OF SARAH DUCHESS OF MARLBOROUGH, AND OF THE COURT OF QUEEN ANNE VOLUME 2 by A. T. Thomson

MARY PORTER GAMEWELL AND THE SIEGE OF PEKING *by A. H. Tuttle*—An American Lady's Experiences of the Boxer Uprising, China 1900

VANISHING ARIZONA *by Martha Summerhayes*—A young wife of an officer of the U.S. 8th Infantry in Apacheria during the 1870's

THE RIFLEMAN'S WIFE *by Mrs. Fitz Maurice*—*The Experiences of an Officer's Wife and Chronicles of the Old 95th During the Napoleonic Wars*

THE OATMAN GIRLS *by Royal B. Stratton*—The Capture & Captivity of Two Young American Women in the 1850's by the Apache Indians

LEONAUR

ALSO FROM LEONAUR
AVAILABLE IN SOFTCOVER OR HARDCOVER WITH DUST JACKET

PLAINS WOMEN *by Lydia Spencer Lane & Lodisa Frizzell*—Two accounts of American Women on the Western Frontier. I Married a Soldier or Old Days in the Old Army by Lydia Spencer Lane, Across the Plains to California in 1852 Journal of Mrs. Lodisa Frizzell by Lodisa Frizzell

THE WHITE SLAVE MARKET *by Mrs. Archibald Mackirdy (Olive Christian Malvery) and William Nicholas Willis*—An Overview of the Traffic in Young Women at the Turn of the Nineteenth and Early Twentieth Centuries

"TELL IT ALL" *by Fanny Stenhouse*—The Ordeals of a Woman Against Polygamy Within the Mormon Church During the 19th Century

TENTING ON THE PLAINS *by Elizabeth B. Custer*—The Experiences of General Custer's Wife in Kansas and Texas.

CAPTIVES! *by Cynthia Ann Parker, Mrs Jannette E. De Camp Sweet, Mary Schwandt, Mrs. Caroline Harris, Misses Frances and Almira Hall & Nancy McClure*—The Narratives of Seven Women Taken Prisoner by the Plains Indians of the American West

FRIENDS AND FOES IN THE TRANSKEI *by Helen M. Prichard*—A Victorian lady's experience of Southern Africa during the 1870's

NURSE EDITH CAVELL *by William Thomson Hill & Jacqueline Van Til*—Two accounts of a Notable British Nurse of the First World War. The Martyrdom of Nurse Cavell by William Thompson Hill, With Edith Cavell by Jacqueline Van Til.

AMERICAN FRONTIER WOMEN *by William W. Fowler*—The Exploits of Dozens of Pioneer Women of the United States.

FRANCES SLOCUM *by John F. Meginness*—The Story of a Quaker Girl's Abduction and Life among the Miami Indians.

MARGARET QUEEN OF SCOTLAND *by Henry Grey Graham*

PERSONAL RECOLLECTIONS OF JOAN OF ARC *by Mark Twain*

WITH THE IMPERIAL CAMEL CORPS IN THE GREAT WAR *by Geoffrey Inchbald*—The story of a serving officer with the British 2nd battalion against the Senussi and during the Palestine campaign.

www.ingramcontent.com/pod-product-compliance
Lightning Source LLC
Chambersburg PA
CBHW021101090426
42738CB00006B/458